NEURONFLASHING
THE POLEMIC

NEURONFLASHING
THE POLEMIC

IRRITATED WITH HUMANITY

LEONARD L. CLARK III, M.A. ED., M.S. PSY

authorHOUSE®

AuthorHouse™
1663 Liberty Drive
Bloomington, IN 47403
www.authorhouse.com
Phone: 1-800-839-8640

Published by AuthorHouse   10/11/2012

ISBN: 978-1-4772-7729-4 (sc)
ISBN: 978-1-4772-7728-7 (hc)
ISBN: 978-1-4772-7727-0 (e)

Library of Congress Control Number: 2012919016

Dedication

To my loving wife Joy, Ayo and Leonard IV "Q"
Leonard L. Clark Jr.
Freida A. Clark
Leonard L. Clark Sr.
Rebecca T. Clark
Douglas R. Bacon Sr.
Audrey L. Bacon
Lamont R. Clark
Jacqueline S. Rodgers
Leila A. Taylor
Family, Relatives, Friends
Jason Hamm

I F ONE WERE to take the time to study the history of the human race, one may well wonder if humanity is a dysfunctional species. The well-known psychoanalyst, Sigmund Freud, taking note of the endless wars, persecutions, and savage oppression humans perpetrate upon one another, commented that; "man is wolf to man". In contrast, it has also been proven that humans are capable of kindness, civility, sacrifice, and in some cases, even unconditional love. Human beings are a complex species and we display both good and bad qualities. What is of concern is to find out the nature of the bad qualities and what of those qualities irritate us. Furthermore, how can we as humans learn to deal with those situations that cause us irritation?

Contents

Foreword

"Man believes what he prefers to be true"
—Francis Bacon

A s an individual who has received many blessings thus far in life, I appreciate the goodness that can be shown from fellow human beings. I only have to reflect on the numerous charities that are formed, the desire of humans to protect animals and the environment, and even the attempts of many to live a morally just, spiritually guided life as proof of the goodness that can be done. Thinking along these lines has led me to the conclusion that all people are not bad. On November 10, 2007, I was the recipient of a kidney/pancreas transplant. Were it not for the prayers of family and friends, the generosity of the family that lost their loved one, and the tremendous skill of the surgeons and medical staff, I would not be in any condition physically or mentally to write this book. In addition, I have been blessed with a stable family structure and supportive friends. This book is the result of many years of internal conflict between my love of all things intellectual and my appreciation for the people and circumstances that have helped me get to this point. From a standpoint of appreciation, I have no right to write a book such as this. From an intellectual standpoint (or one who has an intense interest in the field of psychology), I have an obligation to write this book. I recognize the goodness of humanity, but choose to reflect upon the displeasure I feel with many of the ills of humanity. For all of the positive actions and emotions we can experience, there are those situations, and individuals, who cause us to experience the worst of humanity. Why?

A great number of unpleasant situations exist in the world due to qualities that emphasize the darker side of humanity. One such quality is selfishness. The instinct to be selfish is biologically mandated and is a means of self preservation.

> *"This is a world of fools and rogues . . . tormented with envy, concerned with vanity, selfish, false, cruel, cursed with illusions"*
>
> —Ambrose Bierce

As every human seeks to preserve him or herself, at one time or another, every human is selfish. For those of us who would gladly give our lives for our offspring or other individuals who we love dearly, selfishness is still the motive because we are behaving in an attempt to protect the recipients of our genes and the objects of our attachments. According to Santrock (2010):

> *Psychology's newest approach, evolutionary psychology, emphasizes the importance of adaptation, reproduction, and "survival of the in shaping behavior". "Fit" in this sense refers to the ability to bear offspring who survive long enough to bear offspring of their own. In this view, nature favors behaviors that increase reproductive success, the ability to pass your genes to the next generation*

This behavior is also a selfish attempt to prolong our attachment to specific individuals who feed our need for approval and acceptance. All human beings act selfishly as most decisions made by each individual are made in the interests of that individual. It is also our tendency towards self-preservation that drives our attitudes and behaviors.

Information processing as the basis of our attitudes

Attitudes can be thought of as mental orientations toward people and things. Attitudes about things can make us fearful or they can make us full of disgust. As we can develop attitudes about things, we also develop attitudes about people. It is our attitudes toward people that will be the focus of this book. Humans are likely to possess attitudes about every aspect of their social world. These attitudes can be stable or they can be fluid and subject to change. The extent to which we are likely to be persuaded to change our attitudes depends on many factors, and is based on the ways we as humans process information. Social psychologists state that there are two primary ways in which we process information to form our attitudes. These two ways are *central route processing* and *peripheral route processing.* Central route processing happens when the recipient carefully weighs and thinks about new information and analyzes the stimuli that are presented to form an opinion. The individual who forms opinions using central route processing forms opinions based on the result of logic, the merit of the information, and the power or coherence of the arguments. In contrast, peripheral route processing happens when the recipient involves their feelings and emotions while developing attitudes and processing information. Peripheral route processing is the major way humans select political ideologies (to be discussed later) and is the major cause of human irritations. Thoughts such as how the recipient feels about the information or stimulus, the emotional appeal of the information, and the recipient's biases and prejudices towards the information or stimulus, illustrates peripheral route processing. If an individual's attitude about a co-worker changes, it will be a result most often of that individual's emotions and feelings toward that person, which very often is not based on logic. It can be said that the majority of our interactions with other human beings involve peripheral route processing.

The way we each process information has a direct bearing on our behavior. The influence that an individual's attitude has on his or her behavior can be weak or strong, but what must be understood is the fact that people attempt to maintain an internal consistency with their attitudes. This consistency of our attitudes is what can cause us to become irritated with similar situations even if they occur infrequently. The attitudes we hold oftentimes lead us to become stressed.

The correlation between stress and irritation

Are you stressed? Stress can be thought of as recognition (mentally and physically) by an individual that a threat has the potential to exist or that a threat is occuring. According to Weiten (1986) *"stress is defined as any circumstances that threaten or are perceived to threaten our well-being and thereby tax our adaptive capacities."*

The experience of feeling threatened depends on what events we pay attention to, and how we choose to interpret them. The act of noticing and interpreting various situations is the act of perceiving. The threats we perceive are threats to individual well-being and these perceived threats challenge our self-preservation instincts and cause irritation. The psychological impact of having to confront threats causes stress. As with many endeavors dealing with the human mind, stress and the intensity of stress felt by the individual is based solely on that person's depth of awareness. There are many stressors such as the death of a loved one or the loss of a friend. Although the death of a loved would be conceptualized as a deep stressor to many of you reading this book, not all individuals would react the same way to such an event. Certain events may or may not provide stress to a specific person, but whatever stimulus that is identified by any individual as a major or minor threat to that individual's sense of well-being is a stressor. Situations are appraised as they are perceived, and this act of cognition is fundamental to the process of existentialism. Our primary appraisal of a potential stressor (any kind of situation or stimulus) determines whether it's a threat. If the stimulus isn't perceived as a threat, we go on with business as usual. If a threat is perceived, we engage in a secondary appraisal aimed at dealing with the threat. We may decide to fight, flee, negotiate, or become irritated with our lack of control over the threat.

We as humans all experience stressors that we must constantly adapt to. Whether it is the first day of school, a first date, taking an important exam, or having an annoying relative visit your home. Stressful situation are all around us. It is important to keep in mind the factor of perception. Keep in mind that a stressor is any situation (environmental or mental) that is *perceived* as a threat. Stress has definite biological and physical correlations, but it is the act of perceiving that gives stress its psychological correlations. Due to the fact that stress involves perception, let us discuss the factors that influence the perception of stress. According to Weiten (1986) these factors are:

- *Personality*
- *Coping Resources*
- *Familiarity With The Stress*

- *Imminence And Duration Of The Threat*
- *Perceived Control*
- *Predictability Of The Stress*

Three general types of stressors

It is within the psychological realm of stress that our book presents its arguments. Emotions are linked to stress, and when emotions that are associated with a stimulus are intense, stress levels are greater. According to Turner in *Essentials of Psychology* there are three general types of stressors:

1. *Cataclysmic events*—Any natural disaster (e.g. tsunami, hurricane), the death of a loved one, or any given moment of a soldier in combat qualify as cataclysmic events. If a cataclysmic event is shared and can be dealt with and left behind, it tends not to leave lasting psychological scares. Examples might include coping with a hurricane or tornado, assuming the damage doesn't linger as it has in New Orleans. Ongoing events, like the aftermath of Katrina or a nasty divorce and struggles over child custody, are more devastating in the long run.
2. *Personal stressors*—major life events, like marriage or childbirth are considered personal stressors. You'll notice that both positive and negative events are personal stressors. In the event that cataclysmic events are combined with personal stressors, the result may be Post Traumatic Stress Disorder.
3. *Background stressors*—also known as daily hassles. The car won't start, the dog left a spot on the carpet, waiting in long lines at the store, etc.

Many of the stresses we experience in life are background stressors, and our lack of control over the frequency and duration of these background stressors causes us to become irritated. This work is for the purpose of provoking thought, and it may assist each of us in understanding the reasons why we feel the way we do. We have defined the concept of stress. It is now important to look at the concept of irritation.

Are you irritated? This book will look at and provoke thought about those situations that illicit frequent and common irritations. It is the purpose of this book to present possible explanations that can help to explain the philosophical, interpersonal, and psychological theories behind why certain situations irritate us. The explanations given are not comprehensive nor are they meant to be taken as the sole explanation or even as a viable explanation. The explanations given are presented in the hopes of getting the reader to brainstorm why he or she may feel and react to these situations in certain ways. In any endeavor, the generation of ideas and hypotheses moves the mind forward. Philosophical thinking can uncover many mysteries as well as create new realities.

This work seeks to explain human irritation from the perspectives of a thin slice of average citizens; the irritated teacher, the irritated driver, the person who is resistant to change, and a host of other "life-roles" we find ourselves in on a daily basis that cause us to become irritated in social settings. If any portion of the ideas and explanations proposed in this book resonates with its readers then the author's goal would have been met. Though it offers no solutions for overcoming irritation, it is the authors hope that the presentation of possible explanations might lead the reader to his or her own solutions. In fact, it is the opinion of the author that irritation is natural and healthy, as it means each individual is engaged in his or her day-to-day existence.

The author can be said to be an interested observer of human behavior, similar to H.L. Mencken (1880-1956). Mencken wrote of the misguided deeds of society and was oftentimes irritated with those who chose to perpetuate stupidity in action and belief. To those readers who will perceive this work to be the misconceptions of an idealistic misanthrope, I agree. However, there is one important point to be made: human beings can be glorious creatures when we exercise compassion, love, tolerance, open-mindedness, creativity, and peacefulness. But when these virtues are not exhibited or when these virtues are overlooked, the familiar feelings of intense hatred towards society resumes. It is assumed that many readers will identify with many of the situations presented in the book, and many readers will not. Truthfully speaking, as long as human beings continue to inhabit the earth we will get annoyed and irritated at the actions and behaviors of others. The intent is to encourage the reader to think about those times when stress and irritation occur. If we can understand our anger, just maybe positive realities can be manifested to offset the negativity. As perception is driven by the individual, it is selfish in nature. As humans are self-conscious and able to reflect on the nature and meaning of what it means to be human, we exercise our unique birthrights that separate us from other life forms.

Introduction

I S IRRITATION A manifestation of stress? It is the premise of this book that it is. What is irritation? There is irritation from a physical and biological standpoint, and there is irritation from a psychological standpoint. A physical or biological example of irritation is a skin rash or sun burn. Irritation from a psychological standpoint is cognitive frustration. Our thoughts (perceptions) create the irritation based on how we take in certain stimuli. The website for the Accurate & Reliable Dictionary (2010) has defined irritation as: *the act of exciting, or the state of being irritated; excitement; stimulation, usually of an undue and uncomfortable kind; especially, excitement of anger or passion; provocation; annoyance; anger.* Irritation can also be thought of as the "state of being irritated" and the "excitement of anger or passion." This conception of irritation is the focus of this book. Because every individual processes and reacts to stimuli differently, many experiences can elicit the psychological state of irritation. Modern-day living supplies a never-ending supply of experiences that lead to irritation.

Modern society as a contributor to stress and irritation

Progress has led human beings to a perpetual striving for technological, economic, and cultural advancement (Baines, 1995). This quest for advancement makes day-to-day living volatile and complex. Humans are in a continuous time crunch as each moment of each day must be maximized in the pursuit of survival. This subjective and peer-influenced need to survive, and in many instances advance, is a pre-requisite for maintaining a certain social and economic standard of living. The desire to maintain an acceptable standard of living poses the perpetual threat that others can disrupt one's chances of attaining or maintaining this standard. This threat is the underlying cause of many negative mental states that manifest themselves in our day-to-day interactions with others. The more complex life becomes, the greater is the collective demand placed on each individual. Daily life presents a competition to survive and as a result a sense of haste and fear is created in the modern individual. The modern individual is conditioned to live rapidly and think superficially. There is a certain amount of anxiety felt by most individuals about maintaining economic independence that obliges the individual to keep up social demands and find security in his or her existence. John Baines (1995) further explains the dread of modern life when he states:

> *It is a modern disease in as much as it is motivated by factors pertinent to our time. It is motivated by the growing velocity and complexity of life, the disproportionate growth of culture, the accelerated advance of science and technology, the frenetic activity and agglomeration of big cities, the struggle for life, the speed of communications, music and noise, the insecurity about the future of humanity, excessive advertising and indoctrination, and the deficiency in true human communication*

Introspection or the existential framework as a means of understanding

According to Soren Kierkegaard, introspection can be a great tool in helping us discover the reasons behind our emotional behaviors. Introspection can enlighten us as to why we are irritated. Every individual has a different reality and as a consequence has experiences that are very subjective. People are products of their environment and adapt their behaviors and thought processes to those environments in their own specific ways. The psychological school of Structuralism advanced by the German Wilhelm Wundt in 1879 was one of the earliest views of human behavior. The theory of Structuralism focuses on subjective experience. According to Turner (2010) Wundt became interested in how people responded to a stimulus. A stimulus is anything that causes a response or a reaction of some kind. The stimulus usually involves the activation of the sensory organs: sight, hearing, taste, touch, and smell. Wundt conducted his studies by focusing on the feelings and thoughts of individuals while they were experiencing or remembering particular stimuli. Although introspection can give us tremendous insight into our own feelings, biases, and fears, many psychologists doubt the validity of introspection as a means of gaining valid information regarding behavior. The reason many psychologists doubt introspection is simply because subjective interpretation can not be verified through rigorous testing. Subjective interpretation is inconsistent. Rigorous testing of objective phenomena is the basis of science. The scientific method requires consistent replication and is based on empirical (observable and measurable) data. Objective measures and methods are used to prove or disprove scientific claims that have been offered. In traditional science and in traditional psychology, objectivity is valued. Many scientists would devalue analyses of behaviors solely on the basis of their subjectivity. Many great thinkers and philosophers have developed their greatest philosophical theories relying on the exercise of one's subjective insight. As stated earlier, on such individual was Soren Kierkegaard, and he is sometimes viewed as being the father of existentialism.

All about philosophy (2011) defines existentialism as: *a 20th century philosophy concerned with human existence, finding self, and the meaning of life through free will, choice, and personal responsibility*. Existentialism is the belief that people are searching to find out who and what they are throughout life as they make choices based on their experiences, beliefs, and outlook without the help of laws, rules, or traditions. As such the individual is responsible for all outcomes of the choices he or she makes in life. This is what is called living authentically. Existentialists such as Soren Kierkegaard stress that a person's judgment is the determining factor for what is to be believed rather than by religious or secular world values. A person's subjective perception as the basis of what should be believed stresses the existential tendency to not rely solely on objective reason in the structuring of ideas. Jean-Paul Sartre, the most famous exponent of existentialism, explains that the reason existentialism takes subjectivity as its basic premise, is based on what Descartes has shown; that our immediate sense of our identity is the only truth of which we can be absolutely certain (Law, 2007). Accordingly, the existentialists reject the notion that the exercise of reason and objectivity can be the best method to finding meaning in life. The existentialists believe that each individual's uniqueness occurs in all those moments in life that can't be dealt with strictly by reason alone (this theme will be dealt with more in the chapter on the irritated citizen). The more rational experiences and institutions become; the more abstract and distant they are. The existentialists think that allowing your emotions and feelings to explain reality is important when trying to find answers to the meaning of life. The existentialists believe that being too detached and rational when you ask questions about life is not prudent. Human existence requires active participation with the environment. The more involved and engaged existence is, the more emotion seems to play an essential factor in understanding it. Reason and objectivity can be a good way to analyze things, but individuals are not detached from existence. Favoring objectivity as the sole means to understand life is only getting half of the picture. Objectivity needs to be paired with subjectivity. The existentialists value the subjective interpretation of life, and the way to do this is to pay close attention to your feelings and moods, which of particular concern is irritation.

Nativist and empiricist views influence how we react to situations

Moods and feelings play a primary role in providing insight into the way your existence is structured. Your feelings emerge from your participation with the world and they disclose how you're participating right now in the world. As many situations cause irritation and anger, it is the existentialist who analyzes situations to seek enlightenment. Research suggests two views of how humans perceive the world. These views are the *nativist* and *empiricist* views. The first view is that people are born with a certain predisposition to view the world in particular ways. This view is called the nativist perspective. In contrast, the empiricist perspective argues that our minds are conditioned by sensory experience. In other words, what we think and perceive with the senses becomes our reality. This is a very important point because our subjective interpretations can be flawed, incorrect, or biased. John Locke and many existentialists support the idea of our perceptions creating reality. The political theorist *Niccolo Machiavelli* (1446-1536) can be said to be an existentialist and he held the view that our own human world is the only world in existence, and that we can make of this world what we will. Descartes was another existentialist, and he believed that humans perceive their environments with their minds. The perceptions humans generate via the mind contain two ideas as proposed by Descartes: *first, the senses are part of the mind, not external to it and second, all of our perceptions are driven, colored, and guided by our interests, needs, and biases.* Essentially, our perceptions are driven, colored, and guided by selfishness. This is the major theme of this book: the act of perception is selfish in nature and our awareness of this fact creates irritation with others. Our minds are at work all the time as we perceive information. Our minds are interpreting the world we live in. We are writing on the slate as well as reading what is on it. We are all existentialists.

> *"It is the mark of an educated mind to be able to entertain a thought without accepting it."*
>
> —Aristotle

Irritation with the Actions of Younger Generations

1

"Young people are indifferent to the adult world and to the future, indifferent to about everything except the diversions of toys and violence. Rich or poor, school children who face the 21st century cannot concentrate on anything for very long, they have a poor sense of time past and time to come. They are mistrustful of intimacy because they have been divorced from parental attention, they hate solitude, are cruel, materialistic, dependent, passive, violent, timid in the face of the unexpected and are addicted to distraction"

—John Gatto

A RE YOU IRRITATED because the people in your peer group no longer can relate to the thought patterns and behaviors of younger generations? Do you wish young people had more respect for older traditions, music, and institutions? Do you feel out of place because new music, television shows, and fashions are often offensive and defy your understanding? Are you irritated with young people who refuse to listen to your advice? Many of the causes of irritation with younger generations can be attributed to the traditional cycles of adolescence and the search for identity many young people engage in. But what of the young who don't see the value of any traditional notions of finding their place in the world or of community and society building? What of the young who don't see the value of formulating an identity that can benefit others in addition to just themselves? These are the people in our younger generations who cause great irritation.

Young people do not value opinions outside of their peer group

Young people value peer relationships. Peers exert powerful influences and pressures to conform on each other Rathus (2011). For those young people who have highly involved parents, elders, and/or caregivers in their lives, the experiences given to the young person by these individuals involve many insights into what it means to mature. Much of the irritation we experience with younger generations is due to the fact that as older persons, we offer advice and guidance, but many young people refuse to accept the advice and disregard the advice as useless. Many young people think that older people are "out of touch" and can't understand what they as younger people are going through. Young people are irritating because they attempt to educate older people on the dynamics of their current situation. Young people fail to understand that older persons have "been there and done that" and possess greater wisdom concerning outcomes and ways of handling different situations. The experiences and mind-set of younger people are just that, the mind-set of someone young and much less experienced.

Young people benefit from relating to peers because peers have interests and skills that reflect being part of their respective generation. This phenomenon is the cohort effect and it will be discussed later in the chapter. Because peers differ in personality and circumstances, young people who interact with their peers are able to broaden their understanding of the world (Rathus 2011), however, many older people become irritated because young people value the opinion of peers solely and reject the opinions of concerned adults.

The young brain as different from the adult brain

Research shows the some behaviors of the young mind are natural. Let's take a further look into the mind of the young person. Judith Newman 2010) in her essay *Inside the Teenage Brain* states:

> *In the past few years, research has shown that the brain of a teen really is different. Two technologies—PET scans (positron emission tomography) and fMRI (functional*

magnetic resonance imaging)—have enabled us to study how the brain changes over time. What researchers have shown is that the teenage brain is still very much a work in progress and functions quite differently from an adult's. True, there are areas (particularly those dealing with motor control and hand/eye coordination) that are as well-honed as they will ever be. (That is one reason why your teen can already whip you at computer games.) But there are other areas—not surprisingly, the ones responsible for things like planning ahead and weighing priorities

Research also states that dopamine levels are also not yet at optimal levels during adolescence. Dopamine is the chemical messenger that allows us to do constant triage in day-to-day life, so we can figure out what to pay attention to and what is background noise. Without adequate levels, life can be a disaster. Needless to say, much of the irritation many of us experience with younger people is a result of body chemistry and physiology.

Are we to blame for the behaviors of our young people?

Another point to recognize is the fact that much of the irritation we experience with younger generations is our own doing. On the surface, the irritation experienced by older members of society appears to be justified. Watching young people navigate through their world with what might be interpreted as reckless abandon can create a large amount of angst for the individuals who have walked that same path and want to prevent those same growing pains. Often referred to as the "lost generation", the reaction among many elders to the attitudes and dispositions they often display is that they want everything handed to them and have no appreciation for the struggle necessary to make it in life. While members of older generations are more than likely inclined to think that the condition of young people today is as a result of their own choices. Exploring and analyzing the environment that created such attitudes reveals that the source of the irritation might be of an internal origin. In an attempt to grant future generations the opportunities and experiences that they were denied or had to struggle for, members of an older generation inadvertently created a group of young people who have no appreciation or understanding of the struggle. Growing up in a time when individuals had to fight for basic civil rights, education for all wasn't a given and hard work was the only way to survive, many older individuals sought to spare their descendents the intimate details of living through such a tumultuous time. The nonchalance evident in members of younger generations was a mirror reflecting the job that their predecessors had failed to do. We have spoiled them and caused them to expect instant gratification. Growing up in a time when you had to work for everything you got taught those who had to work for it the value of a good work ethic. While the older generation was learning and appreciating that lesson little thought was given to how that lesson would be taught to future generations as society changed, the economy improved and major advances in technology were made. We are feeling the effects.

Our customs are to blame also. In the culture of America, where "newer is better", this mindset subconsciously influences children to disrespect older traditions. For example, in the Samoan culture, children are taught to respect their elders. At the dinner table, young people usually don't talk; only the "elders" talk, and young people are expected to listen quietly without making a contribution to the discussion. Perhaps many of you feel that this practice limits the thinking skills of the child or makes the child feel like he or she is insignificant, but this is an example of custom, culture and tradition. Perhaps, if American culture across the board put a limit on the importance of input from the young, some instances of disrespect would be diminished.

Erikson's theory of psychosocial development as a key to understanding

There is a conceptual backdrop that can be used to explain the motivations of the young and old alike. This conceptual backdrop is the theory of psychosocial development proposed by Erikson and it can help to explain the disconnect that occurs between younger generations and older generations. Erikson viewed the developmental changes occurring throughout an individual's life span as a series of eight stages. Erikson suggests that passage through each of the stages necessitates the resolution of a crisis or conflict. Accordingly, Erickson represents each stage as a pairing of the most positive and most negative aspects of the crisis of that period. Although each crisis is never fully resolved, due to the fact that life becomes more complicated and complex as we grow older, each stage has to be resolved sufficiently to equip us to deal with new demands made during the succeeding stages of development. Four of Erikson's stages occur during childhood, while the remaining four stages occur during adolescence into late adulthood. The last four stages will be the focus of our discussion as the final two stages of Erickson's theory explain why many older adults find irritation with younger people. Erikson's theory emphasizes the search for identity during the adolescent years and the acceptance of one's path and accomplishments in late adulthood.

The fifth stage of Erikson's theory and the first stage applicable to our discussion is *Identity vs. role confusion (stage 5/8)*. During this stage teens experience the need to discover who they are and to develop a sense of identity. To the casual observer, young people seem to be perpetually in the stage of finding their identity. The crisis of this stage is usually overcome, but it is still a source of irritation for others as the young person finds his or her way. Conflicting identities often lead to role confusion. When teens go through the process of developing a sense of identity, older adults get irritated because young people often fail to notice that older adults often have the best interests in mind of the adolescent. Older adults do not want the teen to make costly mistakes while they are young that will have negative consequences for the individual as the reach adulthood. Due to the fact that the majority of adults have gone through the identity phase of their lives and some can look back in hindsight at certain things that could have been done differently to affect a more positive future, irritation is experienced while trying to guide adolescents from making those same mistakes or while watching adolescents make those same mistakes.

Many of the actions older adults deem as "mistakes" that are made by the young in trying to find an identity involve altering physical appearance, adopting alternate philosophies and lifestyles, and using drugs. These measures are adopted as the teen tries to find his or her purpose, which coincides with the existential goal of living authentically, but the consequences can be detrimental. The adult becomes irritated that the youngster is unwilling to heed constructive advice and warnings.

Intimacy versus isolation (stage 6/8) is the next stage and it occurs during young adulthood. Individuals in this stage achieve intimacy if they're able to open themselves up to others and share feelings and experiences. Isolation occurs when intimacy isn't established. Older adults get irritated with the young during this phase when the young adult experiments with promiscuity or possibly same-sex relationships. Due to the fact that many young adults are at the height of their attractiveness and have a mentality that they can slow down when they get older and that the present is to be lived and enjoyed carelessly, older adults get irritated because they can see the negative consequences of this approach to life (e.g. unwanted pregnancy or the disruption of an education).

Generativity versus stagnation (stage 7/8) is the next stage an individual goes through as they mature further. Generativity vs. stagnation occurs during middle adulthood. The term generativity for Erickson means working to help yourself and others find a fulfilling balance among work, play, and intimacy. In short, generativity is largely about balancing self-concern with concern for others. If your past achievements have been few, moving toward generativity may be difficult. The alternative to generativity is stagnation. Stagnation is a sterile, empty focus on self. Erikson identifies the challenge of middle adulthood as living for yourself or living for the benefit of others and society. Irritation with the young occurs within the older individual who is experiencing this phase of life. The older adult feels the need to perform a debt to society in the form of giving helpful advice to or mentoring a younger person. The irritation creeps in when the younger person does not willingly accept the advice of the older individual, thereby, causing the older individual to feel that they have failed in positively resolving this stage.

Integrity versus despair (stage 8/8): is the eighth and final stage that occurs in late adulthood when the individual assesses whether he or she has lived a life that is truthful to oneself. If that individual has been true to him or herself, he or she can't be false to any other. You live your life as well as you can, owning up to your mistakes, taking responsibility when others haven't, and allowing your gains in life to be of value to both yourself and to others. In a world that encourages competition at any cost, integrity often goes unnoticed. A person in this stage will experience despair if he or she hasn't developed a sense of integrity. The older individual begins to despise younger persons who display no integrity simply because they are faced with the challenge of recognizing that they chose to live with it or the guilt of not having it at all. The older individual is either shocked by his or her "reflection" in the actions of the young person, or jealous of the young individual's ability to develop integrity at such a young age.

The discussion of Erickson's stages is strictly to form a conceptual backdrop for possible reasons why there is a disconnection between older and younger generations and what each individual, whether old or young is going through when perceived by the opposite age range. Having the conceptual backdrop does little to help soften the blow of the perceived actions of the younger generation. The fact still remains that young people oftentimes irritate those who are older.

The infinite amount of time orientation of young people

Young people have no clue about how precious and scarce time is. They waste time in an offhand way. Young people reason that they are young and life is long and they have time to relax. Then one day they realize that the end of life gets closer and they realize that the years have passed. The realization of the finite nature of time and how one has lived one's life is a subjective exercise and as such is existential. When individuals reach old age, and recognize that there is little time left, they become disappointed at the meager accomplishments they have had in their lives. Individuals will recall with dismay and sadness all of the things they had hoped and dreamed and planned to do, but have never done. This could be a consequence of foolishly assuming that life is long and there is time to kill today. Individuals should recognize and confront the impending finality of our lives and take full advantage of the limited time available to us to make our lives meaningful. The realization of those who have grown older and wiser that it is important to take advantages of life's opportunities and not depend on tomorrow fuels the irritation many older people have with the young. Although it is human nature to seek individual happiness and purpose, why do many young people disregard and mock the common wisdom of those who have gone through many of the trials and tribulations of living before? This is why young people are irritating, for older adults can offer nurturance, guidance, and sympathy for the young as they face issues, but in many instances, the younger generation exhibits no mutual respect for the insight or the existence of the older generation. Is this behavior on the part of the young learned? Or is this behavior a natural consequence of being an adolescent or young adult? It is my assumption that the majority of the disrespect is learned. In other words, disrespect is nurture, not nature. This observation causes me great irritation as I am willing to bet it causes many of you irritation. If many of our behaviors are learned from the social aspect of our environment (peers, family, and strangers) why can't positive actions be learned to cancel out the manifestation of the negative behaviors?

The thought processes of many young people echo the arguments put forth by the German existentialist *Martin Heidegger*. Heidegger states that the young feel that by relying on others to show them the way they are living in a non-authentic way. To many young people, living non-authentically creates triviality in their lives. As we continue our discussion, we stumble upon an interesting paradox. It was stated earlier that many young people feel like they are invincible and have time on their side and a lot of living yet to do, yet there are many young individuals who take an opposite approach and ponder the finite nature of life. Young people with an existential mind-set embrace the finite nature of living. They feel that if the individual comes to grips with the short amount of time they have to exist, they would not willingly and uncritically go along with the norms of thought and behavior of the masses simply because they are willingly accepted by others (especially older generations). If I genuinely face the fact that I have only one short life to live, I will want to make sure that it is indeed my life that I live and not that of the mass population. This is the mind-set that correlates to the search for identity that many young people go through.

Why rebellion irritates us

What about the young people whose sole purpose is to rebel just to assert their individuality? What about the young people who feel that they have much time left and feel they do not need to live authentically? What about the young people who hate society and rebel because of a subconscious hatred of their inner-selves? Since time immemorial, the generation gap between old and young has always existed all over the world. The only differences in the expression of the generation gap concern the cultural standards of a particular society and how citizens view their elders in that society. While the older generation, which is experienced and wise, always advises the younger generation about the do's and don'ts and lays down a code of conduct for them to follow, it is the culture of the society that lays down the code of conduct for how the youth should respond. The rebellious youth, who are filled with hopes, desires, ambitions and aspirations, are quick to point out that the elders constantly interfere into their affairs and are always nagging at them. The older generation often compares the younger generation of the present day with the youth of the time when they themselves were young. Adding to the confusion of expected roles older and younger individuals play is the effect of media on the minds of our youth. It is easy to put the blame on the media for having a negative influence on the minds of impressionable youngsters. Evidence has been gathered that the music the young listen to, the computer games the young play, the films, television shows and advertisements the young watch and the books and magazines they read in many instances encourage the youth to rebel against the authoritarian elders.

Why do some young people rebel? There are two possible reasons we will discuss here. One possible reason is that members of the young generation build up resentment. Many young people fail to get the love and affection from older members of their family and their resentment and anger builds up. The second reason is that many young people are taught to rebel. Children learn how to handle relationships through the way their parents and others in society have handled relationships, and if many of these situations, the relationships are strained and dysfunctional. The children learn inappropriate behaviors and many decide to rebel. This theory is further strengthened if the individuals they admire or model their behaviors after are rebellious in nature. For those youngsters who rebel, many of the adults in their lives have failed to talk with them about life, have failed to ask the young person about their fears, struggles, joys, or aspirations, and have failed to offer unconditional love and acceptance. It seems as though many of the young people who rebel are caught in an unfortunate cycle, as the adults in their lives have often been unsupported or unloved when they were young as well. As adults, these unsupported children do not have the tools or the desire to reach out and offer guidance or support to younger people.

The giving of material objects and permission to do things is not enough. Time spent with the young person and heart-to-heart conversation is what is needed. If you do not talk with your child, your child knows that you really do not care about them. Money and gifts do not form love. Love is shown in a relationship where your words and actions show a deep commitment to their welfare. A young person desperately needs this kind of personal care. When it is not present, they are very wary of gifts. One cannot buy love. Furthermore, the older person who has not shown that they really care for the child or has made the young person perceive that they are not loved, sets up conditions for a dysfunctional relationship. When a misunderstanding occurs, hostility quickly arises. Resentment is longstanding and is a result of anger over things that have happened in the past. Each new event further builds upon the old. Usually, the anger just settles down, but it still remains in the dormant state called resentment. More importantly, this resentment distorts how a young person understands various situations between themselves and their parents or any older person. This is the source of much rebellion, which causes irritation in so many older persons.

Not in touch with younger generations . . . the cohort effect

Let us look at the reasons older people or generations seem "out of place" with younger generations. Some of this displacement that older generations feel can be explained by the *cohort effect*. The cohort effect is defined as: similarities in behavior among a group of peers that stem from the fact that group members are approximately the same age. According to Spencer Rathus, in his book, *Childhood and Adolescence: Voyages in Development*; a *cohort* is a group of people born at about the same time. As a result, they experience cultural and other events unique to their age group. Rathus goes on to state *"children and adults of different ages are not likely to have shared similar cultural backgrounds. Today's children are growing up taking iPods and the internet for granted. In fact, for today's children, Jennifer Lopez is an older woman."* Children of past generations also grew up with different expectations about gender roles and appropriate social behavior. As the cultural expectations of different cohorts collide, irritation will result. Are you irritated with the young because you have their best interests at heart and want them to not make needless mistakes in life, or are you irritated because you want to be admired and accepted by the young, thereby boosting your own self esteem?

The Irritated Citizen

2

"When we blindly adopt a religion, a political system, a literary dogma, we become automatons. We cease to grow."

—Anais Nin

M ANY AVERAGE CITIZENS (the author included) have no idea or awareness of the intricate day-to-day proceedings and legal maneuvers that take place in local, state, or national government. The average citizen's ignorance of political minutia leads to the possibility that we can be made to believe any political claim. Negative claims offered by the media, opposing politicians, and opposing political parties are often believed and accepted at face value by supporters of a particular political ideology. This unfortunate situation occurs because the average citizen (as a result of not being privy to information on the inner workings and conversations of day to day political activity), have no way of validating the accuracy of a political claim. Rival political parties, when they feel their political ideology has been misrepresented, feel deep irritation. This feeling of irritation based on political maneuvering is an unfortunate part of being an interested citizen in a democracy.

Are you irritated with individuals who degrade others for not being patriotic enough? Are you irritated with citizens of our nation who yell about cutting taxes, but at the same time complain about our deficit? Does it make you upset when these same individuals bad mouth government programs while receiving many of the benefits those programs provide? Do you become irritated with individuals who are "pro-war" and feel that America needs to show its might and police the entire world? In contrast, do you become irritated by government policies that do not seem to reflect the concerns of the average American? Are you irritated by certain political parties that favor people who have more money than you or people who seem lazy and are looking for handouts? Are you upset with the endless conflicts our nation seems to engage in on the international level when at the surface it seems we have no business? How do you feel about individuals who choose to quote the constitution as binding even when using its principles to cause harm or misfortune to others? These are all concerns in our political realm, and many citizens and many individuals such as you are passionate and irritated with how political policies and discussions play out. Let's take a look at what fuels the anger of the irritated citizen.

Who is the irritated citizen?

The irritated citizen more often than not is a voter and we need to analyze various reasons why people choose to vote. Why do people vote? Voter turnout is essential in a democratic society. It is for this reason that psychologists have joined with political scientists to study the factors that motivate people to vote. If you look at it from a classic rationalist view of costs and benefits, you can argue that it doesn't make much sense to vote. Voting takes time, energy and even money (if you have to miss a day of work to get to the polling place). It also is accepted by man that any single person's vote is unlikely to change the outcome of an election. Nonetheless people do vote and their participation in electoral politics remains critical for the survival of the democratic system. Many social scientists have considered the possible motivations for voting, and there have been many factors suggested. Among the many suggestions for the motivations to vote the role of habit, social pressure, altruism, and even genetics. To come more in line with the tone of this text, the assumption is made that many people vote out of frustration and irritation. Those of us who vote with anger in mind vote with the hope that the politician we endorse will "set things right" and enforce our opinion of how our ideal society should function. That statement "our opinion of how our ideal society should function" is a strong statement that speaks to the selfish nature of our hopes, intentions, and actions. Researchers have conducted studies on voting behavior in families. Researchers have found that the party affiliation of adopted children tended to be similar to that of their adopted parents and siblings. This of course is true for genetically-related children and parents. This finding suggests that party affiliation is culturally transmitted and this finding also reinforces the notion of reference groups and the need for affiliation discussed later in the book. Reference groups and those we care about and "who are like us" most often share "our opinion of how our ideal society should function." Even others in our reference group will not have the exact same opinions. However, the opinions are oftentimes very similar. There is another interesting point to be discussed: when the researchers compared the voting behavior of a large sample of identical and fraternal twins, they found that identical twins were more similar than fraternal twins in regard to whether or not they voted, but no more similar in their choice of candidate. In sum, the research suggests that voter turnout is related to genetics while party affiliation is related to environment, hence reference groups and many times limbic resonance. It is nature if we will vote, but it is nurture who we will vote for.

Origins of our political system: The social contract

Before we begin to examine the issues in politics that cause us to become irritated; it is important to discuss the origins of our political system. One such idea our political system is created under is that of the *Social Contract*. Political philosopher Jean Jacques Rousseau has formulated the idea of the social contract. The basic theme of his idea as quoted by Rousseau is *"man is born free, but he is everywhere in chains."* The idea further explains that people freely join a civil society, but the state then imposes sanctions on that freedom. To be effective members of a society, individuals must agree upon a social contract, which gives legitimate political authority to the state that then protects the individual and ensures policies that work toward the common good. The social contract is the backbone of the American political philosophy. Guaranteed rights such as our freedom of speech and religion are covered in our constitution, but a social contract is the pre-requisite of any such constitution. The social contract is the idea that there is an agreement between free and autonomous individuals who come together to form a civil state. The contract is between the citizens and the government/state.

The state provides protection of an individual's life and property and affords individuals the opportunity to live a life of their own choosing. The citizens fulfill their end of the bargain by obeying established laws and pledging their allegiance to the state. Under the social contract, governments are established to protect the property rights of individuals. Prior to the establishment of government, not all individuals were equally equipped to defend their property claims against others. A civil entity was needed to mediate property claims. This civil entity is the government. By freely consenting to join with others in an agreement with the government, the government was obligated to ensure protection of each individual's property by providing known laws, impartial judges, and swift and certain punishment for property violations. Individuals should be free to live peaceful and secure lives with the expectation that their property rights (body, life, freedom, and possessions) will be respected and protected.

In the United States, individuals are thought to have certain unalienable rights which are natural to the existence of the human being. In his book *Cases and Materials on the Law of Real Property*, law professor Ray Andrews Brown writes:

> *Man by nature of his very existence, is endowed with certain natural desires and claims. Among these are the freedom of his body from injury or restraint: the exercise of his faculties in order that he may obtain the material things essential to his life and comfort; and the possession and enjoyment of the physical things of the world which he has brought under his control.*

Professor Brown mentions the above as part of an explanation as to "Man's natural right to property and how the sate or community in which "Man" may live can override such an individual for the good of the whole society. Brown goes on to state *"organized society also has its own de-facto interests, the most important of which is the preservation of peace and order, which can come in direct conflict with man's natural rights to exist and be happy"*. This is especially true if those natural rights harm others. This brings us to the discussion of fanatics. What can cause irritation with many people are those persons who although they are very patriotic on the surface, seem to want to undermine the true operation of the social contract (e.g. certain political parties who are anti-government spending for the common good and pro-war.

In line with the notion of man's natural rights is the notion of private property. Many would agree that money is a recognizable and efficient example of private property. For many, the earning and spending of money is at the forefront of their consciousness. Many individuals in our society value their money, and those who are political fanatics protest the spending of their money via paying taxes. They protest the "contributing of money" via taxes to enable the social contract to stay intact (remember the aim of the social contract is to cultivate the common good for all members of society). It is the opinion of the author that those who refuse to or who would not want to pay taxes are fanatics. What individuals like this fail to understand is that the social contract (government) needs financial backing. Due to the fact that money is the most recognizable signifier of wealth in our society, those who perform the needed functions to keep our social contract intact need to be paid, just as those who hold the beliefs of the social contact sacred (especially with regards to the protection of private property) want to be paid for whatever they do as a livelihood to provide for themselves and their loved ones.

Issues of taxation causes irritation in some

Let's speak about the issues of taxes. What is taxation? Taxation is what occurs when individuals pay to live in a civilized society or country (back to Locke again). You pay taxes to sustain democracy and opportunity. Very importantly, you pay taxes to use the infrastructure paid for by previous taxpayers; the highway system, the scientific establishment, and even the communications system (Lakoff, 2004). In our present day society, many institutions and establishments are privately funded and managed, but in an earlier time in history, that was not the case. Tax money was how many of these institutions were paid for. According to George Lakoff in his work *Don't think of an elephant: know your values and frame the debate (2004);* the issue of taxation can be thought of metaphorically in two ways:

> *Our parents invested in the future, ours as well as theirs, through their taxes. They invested their tax money in the interstate highway system, the internet, the scientific and medical establishments, our communication system, our airline system, the space program. They invested in the future, and we are reaping the tax benefits, the benefits from the taxes they paid. Today we have assets—highways, schools and colleges, the internet, airlines—that come from the wise investments they made* (p. 25).

Using this metaphor, taxes can be thought of as a wise investment in the future. Lakoff (2004) goes on to illustrate yet another metaphor:

> *Taxation is paying your dues, paying your membership fee in America. If you join a country club ort a community center, you pay fees. Why? You did not build the swimming pool. You did not build the basketball court. Someone has to clean it. You many not use the squash court, but you still have to pay your dues. Otherwise, it won't be maintained and will fall apart. People who avoid taxes like corporations that move to Bermuda, are not paying their dues to their country. It is patriotic to be a taxpayer. It is traitorous to desert our country and not pay your dues. Perhaps Bill Gates Sr. said it best. In arguing to keep the inheritance tax, he pointed out the he and Bill Jr. did not invent the internet. They just used it—to make billions. There is no such thing as a self-made man. Every businessman has used the vast American infrastructure, which the taxpayers paid for, to make his money. He did not make his money alone. He used taxpayer infrastructure. He got rich on what other taxpayers had paid for: the banking system, the Federal Reserve, the Treasury and Commerce Departments, and the judicial system, where nine-tenths of cases involve corporate law. These taxpayer investments support companies and wealthy investors. There are no self-made men! The wealthy have gotten rich using what previous taxpayers have paid for. They owe*

> *the taxpayers of this country a great deal and should be*
> *paying it back* (p.26).

The point I want to make is this: the cutting of taxes effects jobs that support the public good such as: police departments, the military, fire departments, schools, and cultural institutions such as libraries and museums.

To all of those irritated with paying taxes, do you want to cut the police force in your town? Would you like to cut the job of your mailman or garbage truck driver? Better yet, keep cutting government funding of our nation's public schools via cutting taxes, so that teachers will lose jobs and parents will have to teach their own children. It is a fact that many parents prefer to home school their children, but at this present time, families who home school are in the minority and many parents rely on our nation's schools for the purpose of educating their children. It is also a fact that many parents prefer private schools, in which the parents and concerned citizens fund the educations of their students. The point I want to make here is that many parents have neither the money to pay for private schooling nor the time to homeschool because they are out working trying to earn enough income for other life necessities. Just to throw in a bombshell, many parents who may possess the time to homeschool, have neither the inclination nor the intellectual or academic background to even successfully educate their children to successfully compete in today's highly technological information society. Those parents who possess the three attributes of time, education, and money for home or private schooling do not represent the majority in our society. In addition to educators already working innumerable hours because there is an existing teacher shortage, who will provide guidance and structure for the children during the work week if teachers jobs are cut? Cut taxes and let children run wild during their formative years so they will become the new generation of illiterates, rapists, murderers, and serial killers? Since the police force has been cut due to lack of government funding (city and state), who will protect you and your property guaranteed in the social contract from the non-schooled children who grow up to become criminals? The same vociferous members of certain political parties who want to cut taxes also fight for safer streets and more police. Isn't this ironic? I know it is irritating. How will we pay for more police if you do not pay taxes?

To be fair, many citizens don't protest paying taxes simply because they don't feel they have an obligation to pay them, many protest paying taxes because they feel the tax money is not being used properly. An example where this thinking is manifested is in regards to the national debt or deficit. How is it patriotic to not want to pay taxes? Many citizens who are against raising taxes, are the same people who supported the 12 billion a month Iraq War, these are the same people who championed the Bush administration's trillion dollar Medicaid Part D. The same people who championed all the projects started under the Bush administration, now suddenly think raising taxes is not a good idea. What funds will cover all those things they wanted to do? Look at any other war in the history of the United States, taxes were slightly elevated to cover them: WW2, Vietnam, even the Gulf War. Many who protest paying taxes are those who loudly proclaim a "militaristic patriotism." Speaking of American militaristic patriotism, what about the irritation felt for those people who are pro-war and support the need for America to involve itself in the affairs of other nations where we have no immediate reason to engage?(more on this topic later).

As was stated earlier, many citizens protest paying taxes because they feel there is a great amount of waste, fraud, and abuse in so many areas of governmental spending. Many feel the government is bloated and irresponsible. Many are irritated because the cycle of "tax more, spend more" does not make good sense. The issue at hand is what "spend more" refers to. Is it spending more on those services theorized in Rousseau's social contract to facilitate the "common good?" Or is it spending more on our military to make our borders safe? If it is the case with spending to protect our borders, would not some people believe that "spend more" is justified? For those readers who believe that this book is blaming any one particular political party and not the other, keep in mind this interesting bit of information: both parties created national debt, it just so happens that the scapegoat for the whole mess is Franklin Delano Roosevelt. This perception of the welfare state as being the sole creation of FDR creates the cognitive schema that Democrats created the national debt. Unfortunately, this misperception still exists today.

Many citizens agree that we need taxes in order to run a central government, but many are irritated because they feel we don't need taxes to fund all the ridiculous entitlement programs for people who will not work. Many are irritated because foreigners are allowed to come to our country (when it is done legally) and reside for seven years without having to pay taxes, at the same time many are earning substantial incomes. That seven year "grace period" could help our nation decrease its debt simply because the time frame to collect money from certain individuals living in our country has lessened and revenue can be collected earlier. This simple entitlement to foreigners creates irritation with many citizens. Many citizens agree that we needs taxes to fund public schools and fire stations, but many are irritated because they feel we don't need taxes to fund all the ridiculous wars and international conflicts we find ourselves in. When it comes to cutting taxes, which irritated citizen are you?

Advocates of military strength and violence cause irritation

Does being someone who loves the United States mean you have to want to kill others? Continuing our discussions about irritated citizens, let us take a look at individuals who are a prime examples of taking things to the extreme. One such individual is Ted Nugent. We will not speak about his disparaging comments about the president of the United States during April of 2012 (and he calls himself a patriot!). We will speak of casual comments this man has made over the years. First off, Nugent at the time of the writing of this book is a board member of the NRA (National Rifle Association). That is okay, Americans should have the right to protect themselves should a threat develop, but to condone killing as the norm? If you don't understand where I am coming from, let us proceed. Read this quote from Mr. Nugent:

> "The war is coming to the streets of America and if you are not keeping and bearing and practicing with your arms then you will be helpless and you will be the victim of evil."

21

When Nugent speaks of war, who does he feel is the enemy? It can be assumed that his point of reference is to Americans, and what we should do to protect ourselves, but who is the enemy? It is an individual's given right to be nationalistic or even racist, but should people die not because they harmed you, but just because they are different? Nugent also has made this comment about what America should do about the Middle East in the 1990s:

> "We want to go to Saudi Arabia, man, and see if we can't get a four iron and knock people's laundry off the top of their heads. Wear laundry on your head and die, is the basic theme of the Damn Yankees"

Know this for sure, I get extremely irritated with Muslim extremists. I personally would not mind If they all were exterminated off of the face of the earth, and the reason is simple: anyone who wants to kill me and my family just because I am Christian AND I have not caused harm to them personally? They need to die before they get me. I am sure many of you agree. The point I am making here is that there are humans (children and women specifically) who just happen to be Muslim but don't want to kill me or any other Americans. Hey should they die just because they have a certain religion. Being Muslim does not automatically translate into wanting to kill non-Muslims or Christians. It is my opinion that by saying 'wear laundry on your head and die" signals ALL followers of Islam, regardless of whether they are extreme and seek to kill are a just peace loving humans who have no desire to take other human lives. So back to my initial question, does being patriotic (in this case loving America) mean you have to have a thirst for or even an attitude of condoning violence? Speaking of being patriotic, Mr. Nugent refused to fight for his country! In other words, he dodged the draft. His Extract of Registrant Classification Record has been posted many times online. He has admitted to it in interviews. In one of the interviews, he actually explains how he tricked the United States Army into excluding him!! How is this individual patriotic? This just proves the point that people are flexible and only choose to proclaim causes and ideologies when it benefits them. This is one valid reason why irritated citizens who are political fanatics irritate me.

There are some irritated citizens who believe America should show her military strength at all costs, and there are those irritated citizens who believe senseless violence and expenditures of money (financed by raising taxes or increasing the debt) to fight wars is bad policy. There are irritated citizens with opposing views on this issue. Our discussion will focus on the "pro-war" citizen who is an irritant to many. For those readers who can discern the mind-set of the author from this statement, that is fine. I am against violence in any form. Is it un-patriotic to be anti-war? Frankly, I believe it depends who you ask. There are many citizens who are irritated by the fact that anti-war citizens are viewed as unpatriotic. Many citizens express their patriotism by standing against the very conflict that can possibly kill and wound other citizens, as well as increase the debt. The feel that the money for war can be better spend funding programs for the social good. It is safe to believe that many anti-war people love their country just as pro-war people do they just have different ideas about what is best for the country.

Any reasonable American prefers peace, as history has numerous examples of the negative consequences of conflict. It is also the opinion of the author that most people in the world hold the opinion that peace is preferable. In contrast, the irritated citizen who is pro-war does not believe it is always possible to solve conflicts without violence. Even in the life of an individual, this doesn't always work. This is precisely why we have police. There are many instances when a nation has to defend itself. As in the examples given earlier (Pearl Harbor, 9/11). So in the mind-set of the pro-war citizen, fighting skills can stop violence and prevent further violence against our nation and our allies. One blogger via the internet posted a scenario: what you would do if you saw a weaker person being assaulted by a stronger person; would you stay out of it because you are against violence? Would you put yourself between the bully and the victim, as Ghandi would? Or would you try to subdue or scare off the attacker? In the opinion of many citizens it would be wrong to allow people to be victimized when they are unable to protect themselves. This scenario applies to our nation as well. To return back to the irritated citizens who are anti-war, many argue for the implementation of diplomatic negotiations. Many of these citizens question the effectiveness of not trying to negotiate before a military engagement ensues when after many of the conflicts are done, the nations engaged in the fight often become allies. Many citizens feel as though ego and money play a big part in starting wars. Think about this, anti-war sentiment often does not need to be coerced, whereas, pro-war sentiment needs to be coerced. This often requires the use of propaganda. When it comes to revenge for atrocities committed against our nation, (e.g. Pearl Harbor, 9/11) it is easy to be pro-war, but when America is the aggressor and chooses violent conflict in a fight that does not directly involve us, that pro-war sentiment is harder to manufacture. To be patriotic shouldn't mean to support everything the government says or does. Anti-war protest during Vietnam proved this fact, for our nation is founded on free-speech. To be patriotic means to support your fellow countrymen or women such as police officers, nurses, firefighters and even your neighbors. Supporting the government without question is fine if you are a mindless drone, and granted sometimes, the government is right concerning foreign affairs, but history has proven that many times the government can get things messed up. Are you irritated that America may be seen as weak or are you irritated at all of the many maimed, killed, and psychologically damaged Americans war has produced. How is war being patriotic if you are allowing your own people to die? Which irritated citizen are you?

Advocates of dismantling Social Security/Medicare cause irritation

The irritated citizen is driven to frustration by the policies that are discussed and created that clearly are of no benefit to him or her. A prime example of this is the discussion to decrease and eventually do away with Social Security. Social security is the epitome of the social contract is the umbrella to Medicare.

Let us take a minute to delve into a discussion about Medicare. The issue of Medicare is a conversation that occurs frequently in the political spectrum, and it is the cause of extreme irritation in many who are not aware of what is going on. The decisions that are made can have dire consequences for many. Currently there are threats to Medicare and Medicaid in Washington, this fact is well-known to many. What is interesting is the fact that HMO's can use their size to bargain for lower prices on drugs, while the government is forbidden from using it's size to get discounts (Lakoff, 2004). Due to the fact the government is unable to get discounts on the prices of drugs from the pharmaceutical companies: Medicare will be forced to compete with private drug companies after a few years on uneven grounds. The private drug companies will get a twelve billion dollar subsidy (that was once used to fund Medicare) to help attract new patients. The strategy is to lure seniors out of Medicare and into private accounts with the lure of temporary lower drug prices, until eventually Medicare will collapse as more and more people leave (Lakoff, 2004).

There is also talk of putting another nail in the coffin of America's struggling middle class with massive cuts in Social Security benefits and higher taxes for working families. A constant theme in the mind of the irritated citizen is the issue of taxes. Whether you are for or against paying taxes, added frustration is cast on the situation when people who have worked most of their lives paying into the system are not able to reap the benefits of doing so. Keep in mind the reason that structures such as Social Security are even being discussed for possible cuts is due to the enormity of the national debt. Again, this scenario can be seen in the light of how taxes are paid and handled.

Proponents for the cutting of social security are using the language of inflation adjustment. It comes down to a plan to slash Social Security by $112 billion over the next decade, massively increase taxes on poor and middle-class Americans (the same theme again), and let the rich off the hook. It is assumed that this kind of plan could never pass if the public understood it. All citizens of differing political viewpoints would oppose it. What is irritating to the average citizen is the fact that our lawmaking entities of the government (Congress) will not tell the average citizens the specific ways this 'inflation adjustment" will be executed. If our politicians are successful in implementing a plan to cut Social Security, Social Security benefits for an average earner retiring in 2011 at age 65 will be slashed by $6,000 over 15 years. The longer you live, the bigger the cut. What will happen to the children and grandchildren of the present generation? Well, someone born today who hopes to maybe retire at 70 can kiss retirement security goodbye. This is an example of creating policies that are not for the benefit of the average citizen.

This causes us frustration. It is the opinion of the author that wealthy members of our society who feel that they should be taxed less (in proportion to total income) than the average working man or working woman are fanatics. This sentiment also goes out to those persons who may not have comparable income to the extremely wealthy, but support tax breaks for the wealthy just the same. Democracy is an ingenious institution, and as such, the concerns of every citizen should be taken into account, not just the concerns of professional politicians or the rich and influential.

Psychological insights of rival political ideologies

Since the concerns of every citizen are important, let's look at how the ideologies behind those concerns are formed. The popular view is that our two big parties are involved in a clash of ideologies. Democrats stand for equality and greater federal control. Republicans represent freedom and greater state control. Most of us know the slogans and "talking points" of the two parties pretty well by now. Yet while ideologies have traditionally defined our political parties, the real difference may be more psychological than ideological. It may really be one between psychological types rather than political ideologies. The distinction may seem subtle but it is important. It is not the intent of this book to argue the merits of both the Democratic and Republican political parties. However, as this book probes the psychology of irritations as they are perceived by individuals, it is important to analyze the psychology of the two major political parties in our society. The differences in perception and cognition may help explain why we are often irritated with those in the opposing political party. As politics create the political fanatic, so does politics also create the irritated citizen.

From a psychological perspective, the traditional view of Republicans and Democrats suggests that the major difference between the two parties is simply that they are viewed as two different psychological types. One party thinks about issues while the other party feels about issues. It is important to note that this orientation toward psychological types that are characterized by conservatives and liberals are not concrete, set-in-stone truths. Many moderates of either political ideology exhibit both the thinking (rational) approach and the feeling (emotional) approach. It is one of the great issues that cause irritation among thinking citizens who understand that broad generalizations have to be made to increase the stature and identity of each political party. Many of these broad generalizations are based on emotional appeals.

The fact that many appeals are made based on emotion creates the conflict between a "seemingly" thinking Republican perspective, and a feeling Democratic perspective. The cognitive differences in the liberal and conservative mindset are addressed in George Lakoff's The Political Brain. Conservative thought has a moral basis that begins with the notion that morality is obedience to an authority. This authority is assumed to be legitimate and inherently good, knows right from wrong and functions to protect us from evil in the world. This thought process is related to the concept of moral realism as it was introduced into the psychological literature by Jean Piaget. Moral realism as a concept falls under Piaget's Theory of Moral Development. Moral realism or objective reality is a stage of moral development in which the person considers behavior to be correct when it conforms to authority or to the rules of the game (Rathus 2011). Persons who exhibit moral realism perceive rules as embedded in the structure of institutions. Rules and notions of right and wrong are absolute. Rules are the ultimate reality (hence the term "moral realism") (Rathus 2011). It must be stated that the theories of Jean Piaget were formulated to explain the development of children, and moral realism explains the thought processes of children at the age of 5 years old. This theory forms a very similar mindset to certain political fanatics, so it was imperative that it be discussed in this text.

It has been found that many individuals attribute human characteristics to institutions and ideologies. In other words, many people 'personify" institutions and ideologies. The tendency of people to personify is often unconscious, but it occurs nonetheless. Conservative thought is personified in the guise of the "strict father" and in contrast, liberal thought is personified in the stereotyped emotive, empathetic guise of the "nurturant parent" (Lakoff, 2008). Let's look at the strict father vs. the nurturant parent models of political ideology.

The strict father is the moral leader of the family, and is to be obeyed. The family needs a strict father because there is evil in the world and the father has to protect them. Translated in politics, the strict father model explains why conservatism is concerned with authority, obedience, discipline, and punishment. If the reader remembers, earlier in the chapter, we introduced the concept that "patriot" is derived from the root pater which means father. Based on this, it is easy to see the subconscious correlation between patriotism and the strict father model. Lakoff goes on to state that in the strict father family, for the father to know right from wrong, there must be an absolute right and wrong with absolute categories. This concept offers another insight as to why those persons who are irritated most with "those not like us" tend to be conservative as persons with absolute perceptions of right and wrong are least resistant to accept others, especially if the others exhibit characteristics that are deemed wrong. In the strict father family, it is assumed that the father merits his authority. Through much conservative rhetoric, hierarchies of power and wealth are justified on "merit". It is the belief of many that subscribe to the strict father mind-set that CEOs make so much more money than other employees because they deserve too. The strict father orientation also welcomes competition. Competition builds discipline. Without it, no one would have the incentive to be disciplined and morality would suffer. Because of the fact that not everyone can win in a competition, only the most disciplined people are worthy of the victory (whatever the victory entails). Winning in this mind-set is a sign of being deserving and morally superior. Competition is the basis of capitalism and it is easy to see how individuals with this mind-set oppose political orientations that entertain the idea of helping the less fortunate.

While discussing the strict father model, it is easy to spot the correlation of morality (mainly as it applies to religion) and the conservative political ideology. For the sake of being objective and non-stereotypical, it can be said with certainty that a great number of the supporters of the conservative political ideology are Christian fundamentalists. Lakoff asks the question: why are fundamentalist Christians conservative? He goes on to explain that fundamentalist Christians view God as the ultimate strict father. Lakoff states:

Obey my commandments and you go to heaven; if not, you go to hell. Well, I'll give you a second chance. You can be "born again." Now obey my commands (as interpreted by your minister) and you go to heaven; otherwise, you go to hell: authority, obedience, discipline, punishment. Note that "individual responsibility" is a hallmark of this view of religion—it is up to you and you alone as to whether you get into heaven

An important point needs to be made at this point, many liberals are fundamentalist Christians. This text does not want to advance the idea that only fundamentalist Christians are conservative, many Christians, whether conservative or liberal, hold fundamentalist views. The difference lies in their level of support of the notion of Christian service and helping out those who are in need.

The contrasting perspective, which is the basis for many liberal policies, is the Nurturant Parent Model. This political ideology stresses the role of empathy, responsibility for oneself and others, and the strength to carry out those responsibilities. As opposed to the strict father model, the nurturant parent model is a personification of a two-parent household, with each parent/gender taking on equal responsibilities. It can be said that this mind-set fuses both the "feminine" qualities of care and empathy, with the "male" qualities of rules and discipline. In the political realm, we see the nurturant parent model manifested in the politics of empathy. Lakoff explains: "Here we see the politics of empathy emerging in the family. When mapped onto the nation, the result is the progressive politics of protection, empowerment, and community."

Aside from the human tendency to personify ideologies, the main point of this chapter is this: the most irritating aspect of being an informed and concerned citizen is the realization that people use their emotions and party allegiance to influence their political beliefs and actions. People do this instead of thinking about compromise. People do this without thinking in depth about the issues at hand. Are you irritated with other citizens who do this? Or are you one of the individuals who create the irritation? We will begin by discussing the formation of political ideology. Research suggests that many people construct their political ideology based on their subjective moral compass (there's that theme again of subjectivity). Cognitive scientist George Lakoff states *"politics is about moral values. Every political leader presents his or her policies on the grounds that they are right—that is, they are moral."* In the past, the idea of morality as the determining factor for political actions was advanced thinkers such as Henry David Thoreau. Thoreau argues that it is every citizen's duty to act according to their morals, even if that conflicts with what the government dictates. Many right-wing extremists hold this same opinion. Getting back to the issue of morality, research has suggested that humans possess five categories of moral concerns. Often, these moral concerns are consistent even across different cultures. These categories of moral concern are:

- *harm/care*
- *reference group/loyalty*
- *authority/respect* *
- *purity/sanctity*
- *fairness/reciprocity*

Betrayal of one's community is likewise judged negatively across cultures. A respect for authority and the value of fair treatment for members of the community also appear to be cultural universals. The purity/sanctity category relates to the emotion of disgust and involves moral judgments about dietary laws, sexual practices, urination, defecation, and other similar issues. Having discussed the universals of moral concern across cultures, we are brought to the question: do political liberals and conservative differ in the way they understand morality? It is the opinion of the author that liberals and conservatives do not vary in the way they understand morality, but that liberals and conservatives vary in the degree to which certain moral concerns are dominant in their lives. Having stated this, it is of little surprise that attitudes toward the five categories of moral concerns may also influence political beliefs. In other words, political conservatives and liberals may emphasize different categories of moral instincts from one another. In a large website-based study, researchers have found that political liberals valued harm/care and fairness/reciprocity more than conservatives did, and conservatives valued authority/respect, reference group/loyalty, and purity/sanctity more than liberals did. The fact that conservatives value authority/respect more that liberals will be discussed further later in the chapter. These differences held even after accounting for the effects of age, gender, education and income. This study helps us understand why people with equally strong moral convictions may vehemently disagree on political issues such as abortion, capital punishment and flag burning. From our previous discussion, it is obvious that many moral concerns can be said to be universal, but let us look at the idea of rationalism and reason as universal attributes.

According to Lakoff (2008) America was formed on the principles of the Enlightenment. The idea of Enlightenment is that humans utilize universal reason in all of their affairs and this capacity for logic and reason is what makes humans great. The idea of reason and rationalism extends to politics, and this use of reason and rationalism in politics forms the background of the American Democracy (along with the social contract). In his book, *The Political Mind: A Cognitive Scientist's Guide to Your Brain and its Politics*, George Lakoff gives us an astounding list of rational views that explain how the link was made between universal reason and democracy:

- *Since all people have the capacity for reason, we can govern ourselves, without bowing to higher authorities like kings or popes.*
- *Reason makes us equal, and so the best form of government is a democracy.*
- *We use reason to serve our interests, and so an optimal government would serve the interests of all.*
- *Since we all have the same reason, the same laws can apply to all; thus, we can be governed by general, rational laws, not individual whims.*
- *Our inherent rational nature accords us inherent rights and freedoms.*
- *Government should be dedicated to the rational interests of all citizens, and must be structured so that no authority can overwhelm them.*
- *Reason contrasts with blind faith, and so government should be separate from, and independent of religion.*

- *Science is based on reason, and so our government should recognize, honor, and develop scientific knowledge.*
- *Therefore, a government committed to reason will be a democratic government.*
- *When democratic values are violated, it is reason that must be restored.*

The ideals of reason as they once related to the creation of our democracy have served us well. However, we need to discuss how in today's society, many of our political behaviors are influenced by our emotions. Many actions are better formulated using reason and rationality, but it is not good to cancel out emotion when dealing with politics. If politics followed the strict mandates of reason, politics would be universally rational. This is not the case. If citizens were made aware of facts and figures, they would naturally use reason to enact the correct conclusion. This is not the case. In the rational sense, voters would calculate which policies and programs are in their best interests, and vote for the candidates who advocate those policies and programs (regardless of political affiliation, race, or gender). Voters don't behave this way, they vote against their obvious self-interest, they allow bias, prejudice, and emotion to guide their decisions, and they vote based on their political party affiliation.

> *"Ideology isn't driving the dynamic in Washington. It's our desire to stay in power."*
>
> —David Axelrod

Psychological research has suggested that those who favor a conservative ideology are fundamentally more anxious than those who favor a more liberal ideology (Warren, 2012). Because conservatives can be thought of as more anxious, they typically desire stability, structure, and clear answers. These qualities are reflected in the platform of their chosen political party (Warren, 2012). With the increasing complexity of modern life, and the resulting difficulties the average citizen is faced with, those who support the conservative mind-set find a way to keep their anxieties to a manageable level (Warren, 2012). What the aforementioned statements suggest is the possibility that the more safe and stable an individual feels, the more likely he or she is to adopt more liberal views.

Research has shown that Individuals vote along party lines even if they are unclear of the issues at hand or even if they are unsure of the candidates who are running. When it is time to enter the voting booth, it only matters where the names fall (are they candidates for my party or the *other* party?) I have been presented with this issue myself. During the most recent General Assembly elections in my city, a good friend of mine called me to see if I was going to vote. Regrettably, I told my friend that although I consider my self a dutiful citizen who votes regularly, I was not planning to vote in this General Assembly election. I informed my friend that I was not aware of the candidates and not aware of the platforms each proposed. My friend then stated "it does not matter, just vote Republican." That statement caught my attention. It was a directive to just vote the party line. To vote the party line regardless of the issues or candidates made me realize just how out of touch many of us are with the real issues. Voting to many of us is to keep our political party in office. Even if opposing candidates from opposing parties have intelligent, coherent, well thought-out platforms, many of us will refuse to give the ideas any thought because it has been proposed by the *other* party. This thought process causes irritation because the negative behaviors and policies of a particular candidate are used as the total thought of an entire party, and the positive policies that either political ideology has is not given exposure. This creates and contest of ideologies with only a simple, unsophisticated analysis of the issues.

Although voters are influenced by morality as discussed earlier, they still argue with others about values and priorities. Enlightenment reason and rationality does not account for actual political behavior. The reader may ask: what does all of this talk about Enlightenment rationality and emotion have to do with being an irritated citizen? The point is this: our emotions and morals are influenced by our self-interest and biases. These emotional biases affect our political behavior which influences us to select certain political parties, adopt certain political beliefs, and become irritated with those who don't adopt our emotional mind-set. Rationalism alone is no factor in the scheme of our politics. It is good to understand this fact. It is a more accurate statement that both rationalism and emotion play an important role in political decisions. Rationalism and Emotion should work hand-in-hand. What causes irritation is the fact that emotion takes the dominant role in political decisions, and people become irritated with others based on emotional guidelines. Our emotions and values decide which political affiliation we choose to support.

It is not only every four years or when there is a president or congressional majority that many don't agree with that politics takes center stage. It is also during the times when our self-interests are not reflected in the policies that are enacted. When politics do take center stage, each of the major political parties proclaims their virtues to the public. These proclamations are made to appeal to the masses. This very fact can cause irritation among citizens who are concerned with deep issues and not with the propaganda each party spouts. This is one of the reasons many irritated citizens choose "independent" affiliations and independent candidates for political office. During election time, the perpetual background hum of politics gets crafted into short, sharp advertising sound bites.

> *"To read what Thomas Jefferson (and the rest of our Founding Fathers) believed, is to understand why we must get back to abiding by the Constitution. The problems we face today are, for the most part, because we have allowed immoral and dishonest politicians, and a Supreme Court that legislates its own preferences, instead of upholding the Constitution, to work unopposed. When a sinking America is forced by its Patriots to return to our Constitutional roots, it will right itself."*
>
> *—Ron DuBois*

Irritated With Technology:
Arguments from the Luddite

3

"The more humanity advances, the more it is degraded."
—Gustave Flaubert

PERSONALLY SPEAKING, THE thoughts I have regarding technology mirror those of the Russian existentialist novelist Fyodor Dostoyevsky. He held the belief that the creations and advances in science and technology have the potential of possibly destroying civilization at the same time as it advances it. Imagine you are walking around a large suburban shopping mall. You are Christmas shopping for your niece to be exact. Your niece is a tween and you are in the young ladies apparel section of Macy's with your wife. Your wife is searching for the perfect outfit and as the two of you circle around with a purpose, but with no idea etched in stone as to what to buy, you come across the winter apparel section (remember it is December). You are looking at the vast array of hats, scarves, and gloves with their stylish assortment of colors and textures. As you pick up a pair of gloves you notice that the fingers are cut off. Where the glove would normally cover the entire palm/knuckle area and each of the five fingers, you pick up a pair of gloves in which the sections where the five fingers would be inserted are cut off! I will admit that people think differently, and that is one of the basic assumptions that drive the arguments in this book, but my personal opinion is this: what good are gloves (placed in the winter apparel section) that leave your fingers and fingertips exposed to the elements? I asked my wife if she knew the purpose of gloves with the fingers cut off, she replied that she did not. At this point, my curiosity got the best of me, I tracked down an associate clear on the other side of the store and asked her to follow me to the section where the gloves were displayed. I asked the young lady if SHE knew why the gloves were made this way. The associate was well aware of the purpose of the gloves. She informed me that the gloves are made that way to allow wearers of the glove to text! You heard me right, many of you may have already been aware of this fashion trend in which the act of text messaging via cell phone, PDA, etc. has created a demand for gloves that will allow the wearer to text. It may be just me, but if your hands are cold (which would be the reason you purchased the gloves in the first place, you want them to be warmed. It may be just me, but can't the individual wait to find a location in which it is warm enough to take the gloves off completely before he or she engages in the act of texting? Is it that important to respond to the text at that moment? How about just talking on the phone? That way you can keep your gloves on? Maybe I'm out of touch. Go figure.

During that same shopping excursion, my wife and I stumbled across a t-shirt in the little girls section. The ages and sizes of the clothing were for girls aged 2-6 years. My wife picked up one shirt that caught my attention. It was a pink number with gold and white lettering that stated "born to text". This was the saying actually silkscreened across the front of this shirt! The shirt was made for a 4 year old, and the shirt is proclaiming born to text? I am irritated. Many four year olds do not know all of the letters of the alphabet, nor do they have a social network where they need to text. Mom and dad do just fine communicating through the art of vocal speech. I am irritated. Let us move forward.

Are you irritated with gadgets and gizmos that require a tremendous expenditure of money only to become outdated or obsolete weeks later, or need replacing or repair due to mechanical malfunctions? Are you upset with children who no longer use their creativity and no longer get exercise due to video game consoles or computers in the home that make going outside to play to them seem a chore? Are you worried about the constant changes in technology that have made certain livelihoods irrelevant, which has caused the loss of many jobs? Do you feel that technology has made human interaction a choice rather than a necessity? For the person who is irritated with technology consider this: science and technology advance faster than human beings can bear. This is what is meant by Karl Marx when he states that "*the superstructure of a culture (religion, arts, politics, values, and law) evolves slower than the economic (technology and science) infrastructure of a culture.*"

Technology drives obsolescence

According to Baines (1995) the advances in the economic and technological infrastructures may become a serious threat for the future if appropriate measures of control and education are not taken. We know that any technical advance forces the individual to make an effort of adaptation that requires a certain period of time. If the changes are too fast and numerous, then the individual does not manage to adapt quickly enough and is left behind. This scenario is a cause of irritation and the intense and continuous effort of adaptation may produce distress, neurosis, anguish and other debilitating conditions.

Call me a "dinosaur", but I am an individual who is resistant to change. This resistance to change can be attributed to my longing for security, but part of my resistance to change is driven by the awareness that advances in technology some make time-honored crafts and skills obsolete. While surfing the internet (it may seem ironic based on the subject matter of this chapter, but I do use the internet), I came across an opinion poll posted on an employee only inter-office website on October 19, 2011. The poll posed a question which states:

"*The writing is on the wall for cursive. Now, 44 states no longer mandate teaching cursive in classrooms. What do you think?*" The responses offered and the percentages of answers given were as follows:

44%—*cursive is still relevant*
48%—*cursive is a good skill to have, but not essential*
8%—*who writes? I only use a keyboard*

It is the last category of responses that irritates me. It is the 8% who responded "who writes? I only use a keyboard" that causes me great concern. Granted, 44% responded that they felt cursive writing still has a place, but to those who don't engage in the act of handwriting at all, what is going on? It appears that technology is making handwriting obsolete as more and more individuals type emails, text messages, and talk (via cell phone). I will admit that traditional writing presents issues such as legibility (as many people have less that neat handwriting), and time. Many people simply do not have the time to sit down and write out text in long cursive or any type of handwriting for that matter. The issue at hand is that when traditional skills become lost, the world loses yet another beautiful human expression at the expense of advanced technology and speed. Think of all the mass produced items that are ubiquitous in our society. This "mass produced" ethic is what fuels the passion some have for handmade clothing, crafts, and clothing. This passion has a counterpart in those who prefer an organic lifestyle. Individuals such as this realize that the mass production of food items has increasingly relied on technology. This technology often times is detrimental to the health of the consumer and to the heath of the live animals used to produce the food item. Will our pre-school and kindergarten age children begin to type their names on a keyboard rather than learn to write their names by hand?

New dangers are introduced by new technologies

It has been proven that technology can and does benefit mankind tremendously (e.g. the internet, cell phones, home security systems, medicine) but when technologies expand, there are always trade-offs that negate the benefits of what the technology was created to achieve. The two previous examples given of the internet and cell phone are great illustrations of this paradox. The internet allows users to connect with others all over the world, pay bills, shop, and even develop and maintain relationships. It is safe to say that the ability to do these things can be seen as a great benefit to mankind. The internet has given millions of people greater flexibility in choosing how they live and structure their lives.

With the advent of the internet comes, inevitably, the negative trade-offs. Child pornography, viruses, and internet scams that rip people off are some of these tradeoffs. There have always been people out to deceive and do harm to others since time immemorial, but the point I am making here is that the structure of the internet amplifies the negative consequences worldwide in seconds. The hit television show "To Catch a Predator" on MSNBC has only been made viable after the invention of the internet. Although child pornography has existed unfortunately for decades or longer than the invention of the internet, the proliferation of these and other associated crimes has skyrocketed since the internet's birth.

What of instances of robbery and murder that have been facilitated by the internet? "Craigslist.org" is an online site where people can offer items and services for sale. This is a good thing as many items are hard to locate in standard retail or simply for the fact that many of the items on Craigslist are deemed more affordable. Also, many listings involve services that may not be available in conventional avenues. During the summer of 2012, I watched a local news broadcast in which many individuals complained of being robbed as a result of looking to purchase items on Craigslist. The individuals in question set up appointments with the sellers of items and upon arriving at the agreed upon location, the "seller" proceeded to rob the purchasers of their money (many times at gunpoint). Need I mention the murders that have occurred as a result of such sites? It is not the aim of this book to suggest that the internet is the sole cause of such crime, or that robberies and murders don't occur in everyday life in spite of technology, the point being argued here is that the internet creates another avenue for crimes of robbery and murder to occur, and the scope of the crimes are not limited to individuals in the same geographical area, as some persons have travelled across states to obtain services offered via the internet.

The internet is one of the most influential technological devices ever created, but another tradeoff is its tendency to promote laziness. Why go from store to store or from library to library searching for that needed item or book when you can just surf the net and "click". Instead of writing letters with beautiful handwritten, people send quick emails filled with misspelling, grammatical mistakes and abbreviations. Tech abbreviations used for emails and text messages have begun to affect young students as many are unable to differentiate correct English from the language created via internet and cell phone text messages. For many individuals who strive to develop meaningful conversation, cell phone text messages create irritation. Without a doubt, the internet has both positive and negative effects on modern society.

Technology limits instances of genuine personal interaction

On a personal level, my wife and I try to engage our children in conversation on various topics. We do this to promote their intellectual development, but also to let them know that we value their opinions. One of the major ways to develop a close relationship with your children is to have open heart-felt discussions with them on any number of topics. On Saturday mornings, we often sit down to breakfast and talk about current events and philosophical ideas. Many times, the television is on in the background. The conversation is great, but as soon as a text message alert appears on their phones or their favorite video or television show pops up on the television screen, the discussion is ended. Although we could very well plead our case and have our children turn off all televisions and phones until our discussion is over, we allow them to carry forth with their preferred distraction. The personal example illustrates the advances in technology but it also demonstrates the downside. In the past, there were no cell phone and text messaging was still science fiction. Television did not have so many channels to choose from so that if you were not engaged in a particular show to begin with, chances are, there would be no other programming available to spark your interest at least until later in the day.

Back to the issue of cell phones; humans have always had a need to communicate with others as humans are social beings. What if your grandmother's car just blew two tires on a rural dirt road? Don't worry; she can pick up her cell phone and call AAA or a trusted friend or relative. One of the world's most ubiquitous technological marvels is the cell phone. The cell phone can either be the answer to your prayers or a major pain in the butt. The chances or irritation are many. Like it or not, the cell phone is here to stay. While this technological device positively affects society by providing instant communication, it also dehumanizes relationships and threatens an individual's right to privacy.

One positive effect of the cell phone on American society is its ability to provide instant communication. First, the device is invaluable to car owners who possess older or functionally-challenged vehicles. Nothing makes a driver with an old unreliable car happier that being able to call AAA for a tow on his or her phone and knowing that a tow truck will arrive within minutes. Second, cell phones help keep parents and their children in touch. For example, at a minute before midnight the parents of a teen or pre-teen can call their child's to make sure they are safe and sound and to demand that they arrive home shortly. Third, if a loved one is half-way around the world, family members can pick up the cell phone and check in and deliver special family moments to the away relative or rest their fears knowing that the relative is okay. In summary, the cell phone's ability to allow anyone to be reached at any time soothes America's collective psyche.

In contrast, the cell phone has its disadvantages. These disadvantages are often the very instances that cause irritation. There is a paradox that occurs within the milieu of the cell phone. The technological device that can bind society together trough instant communication can also destroy those binds through the process of dehumanization. Whether you are stuck in a horrendous traffic jam or relaxing in a romantic restaurant, people will more than likely be talking on their phone or texting on their phone. Just walk down any city street or inside any mall and in less than a few minutes you will observe hundreds of people, men women, and children, ignoring each other as they carry on conversations with others on the phone. Literally, cell phones are replacing living, breathing, human beings as the actual physical presence of that person is not required or even desired in deference to the phone. The act of texting has made this fact even more explicit. It seems that cell phones are ne of the technological advancements that removes the "human" element from society.

The cell phone threatens an individual's right to privacy. There are many times when private conversations between husbands and wives, lawyers and clients, doctors and patients, are overheard by others when these persons choose to speak while on the cell phone in open public spaces. Because people in our society are constantly on the go and it seems that time is at a premium, people choose to talk anywhere about the most private of concerns, and often these conversations can be heard by others who have no right or desire to be privy to such. Also, how many times have you been irritated by having to hear the conversation of others? How many times has your meeting, movie or lunch date been disrupted by someone answering their phone and beginning to talk (oftentimes loudly and explicitly) about the most trivial issues that could have been done at another time. Irritation occurs when technology causes an infringement on others (have you ever been irritated with someone talking extremely loud and behaving in a very animated fashion while in line at the grocery store?) This scenario could not have happened 50 years ago when the only way to speak with someone was on a land-line phone which required a designated building (home or office) and a physical wire. No conversation or location is too sacred for the cell phone. Due to the fact that a great percentage of persons in the world use cell phones, the word privacy will soon disappear from our vocabulary.

For the parents of young children or elderly parents, for the individuals who are broken down on the highway or are attacked on the street, for the individuals who are trying to locate friends or loved ones in a crowded public place, for those trying to find directions while in transit (and don't own a GPS system) cell phones are obvious life savers. The benefits of cell phones can be said to far outweigh the costs, but costs there are. With cell phones come texting, and unfortunately some decide to text while driving. No further explanation is needed to account for the deaths and injuries caused by texting while driving, for although car accidents has always occurred since the invention of automobiles, the specific malady of accidents caused while texting is solely correlated with the technology of cell phones. As technology benefits us, it also can put us in peril. Irritation with technology can occur when individuals realize that some individuals fail to use common sense and allow the fascination and prerequisites of the technology to override cautious behavior. Irritation can occur when technology that many of us have grown accustomed to is deemed obsolete. Then in order to enjoy those things again with the new technology, tremendous amounts of money have to be spent (e.g. vinyl records, cassette tapes, videotapes, compact discs).

Technology's effect on behavior in the workplace

Advances in technology have also ushered in a lot of advantages for business applications. Phones for audio conferencing and applications sharing software have definitely provided improvements in the way people do business. Many individuals find themselves irritated with the "culture of technology" that has been created in the world of work. The career website Activist (2011) has listed many complaints that individuals in the world of work have listed as specific irritants:

- *Losing the verbal communication and social skills—there is no reason for being bombarded with emails from someone who sits directly in front of you. Instead of abusing email communication, stand up and walk over to your colleague. You can even get a little exercise from walking a few paces.*
- *Using Instant Messaging to let someone know that you are sending them an email—this is excessive and distracting to the recipient. Popping a chat message to say that an email was sent to them does not mean that they will read it ASAP. So why waste effort and time sending an IM anyway?*
- *Placing every one (especially the boss!) on the distribution list—ever heard of company policy on information disclosure? Only send the email to pertinent people. Do not include those who do not really need the information.*
- *Sending text messages while in a meeting—this situation is highly annoying and distracting, especially for the presenter. If you are in a meeting, turn your mobile off or put it on silent mode (without vibration) so you can focus on the issues being discussed and no one will be distracted by a constantly ringing or vibrating phone.*

There are so many conveniences that technology can bring and it has made everyday living so much easier. But we must never forget that too much dependence on them can also impair some of our social and professional skills. Always be on top of developments. Do not let new gadgets consume you at the risk of losing your appreciation for the simple ways and things in life. You may risk irritating someone.

The Irritated Teacher

4

"Ideal teachers are those who use themselves as bridges over which they invite their students to cross, then having facilitated their crossing, joyfully collapse, encouraging them to create bridges of their own."

—Nikos Kazantzakis

ARE YOU DISMAYED over the state of education in our nation, as some reports have stated that Americans are 25th among westernized nations in regards to the education of our youth? This chapter highlights those of us who are irritated with the current state of public education in our nation. Although many of the topics discussed in the chapter are applicable to children of all socio-economic backgrounds and those who attend public, private, and/or charter schools, the focus of the polemic is on public schools because public education is guaranteed by our government and the majority of children educated in our society are educated in public institutions (one of the reasons we pay taxes). Having stated this, the point remains that educating our future generations can cause tremendous amounts of stress and irritation.. Are you irritated with the number of teens dropping out of school? Do you become frustrated when all the blame of our current state of education is placed on the teachers and not the parents who should shoulder some if not most of the responsibility? Are you upset that many students don't care if they receive a good education which gives them greater advantages in being a contributing member to society? There are many issues in our society faces regarding education, and we will look at some of them.

Demographics may be a factor in causing some irritation

Speaking with an educator who works in an urban high school, the conversation focused on the many challenges an educator must face when teaching in this demographic. Many children in the urban demographic face many challenges that would seem to not allow for a successful attainment of an education. Many children come from broken homes, many of these children have no family members who value education, many children (teens in particular) are faced with having to raise and support younger siblings or relatives. Many students are parents themselves, and have the added responsibility of providing adequate necessities for another life, along with trying to attain some semblance of an education. Many of these children have parents who not only value education, but are verbally abusive and their life experiences are so limited that they effectively cripple their offspring educationally and socially. I am not suggesting that no parents are concerned about the education of their children. In fact, many of the parents who have not completed their educations nor have substantial employment are concerned about the progress and grades of their children. This concern may be driven by the realization that without a good education or a job, it is very tough to exist. Many of the parents who are under-educated and under-employed do not want this same struggle to happen to their children. The problem that causes irritation among many educators is the fact that many of these parents look to the teachers as the "saviors" of their children. The teachers are expected to be the giver of knowledge. Many parents are so ill-equipped knowledge wise (that is to say academically) that there is no checks and balances structure in the home environment that the parent is able to create to gauge the validity of concepts being learned in school.

To make matters worse, there are some parents who, because of a lack of social graces and decorum, model a negative and ill-fitting personality for their children. This type of personality is often selfish, materialistic, and physically and verbally aggressive, and the children of these parents behave the same way. How can the children of parents who exhibit these traits possibly get a good education and more importantly, change their mind-sets and behaviors to facilitate successful learning and social interaction?

The previously discussed life situations are real. And they occur with startling regularity in many of our nation's public schools. To the same extent as the aforementioned situations can hamper and downgrade the learning environment, they also cause irritation in the educator who has to enter into this environment on a daily basis. One of the major causes of irritation for teachers is the children who will not learn and choose not to learn because they display a "don't care" attitude towards learning in particular and a nihilistic attitude towards life in general. The teacher I spoke with states that so many children in the present generation (those born after 1990) do not care about school or the effect no education will have on their futures. It can be said that peer pressure is a major factor in students not wanting to succeed as many teens fear being called "nerd" but the situation is much more complex than that. There is another label that many students in the urban demographic fear and that is the notion of "selling out" or worse, being signaled as someone who "thinks they are better" because they value their life and well-being. It is this mind-set that in my opinion merits a deeper inquiry.

Self-concept is a term used in psychology to describe the way an individual feels about and values their unique identity in the world. What causes the self-concept of some individuals to be so low that they view themselves as worthless and therefore education is of no viable concern in their day-to-day existence? The answer to this question can be analyzed using the nature vs. nurture debate that exists in many branches of psychology. Nature vs. nurture deals with whether an individual's personality and behavior is shaped by innate, biological causes or if that individual's personality is shaped by the environment. Accepted research states that a person's personality is shaped by both the environment and their genes. Oftentimes, the genetic markers for that person (nature), influences how the person will adapt or react to his or her environment. It is the opinion of the author that with regards to education and the low self-esteem displayed by many of these students, the issue is one of both nature and nurture. Nature will determine if the child has the innate capacity to learn, for example if the child has mental retardation or a low intelligence quotient(IQ), but nurture are those variables that can enhance even these factors as well as make the "normal" student learn to the best of his or her ability. It is the opinion of the author that the nurture side of the controversy has greater influence on why teachers feel irritation. Students with special needs (mental or physical) should be addressed by specialists trained to deal with the challenges children such as this present (more on this later in the chapter). Whether it is by design or it is by error, the majority of students in our public schools are deemed "normal". Because of this, the special training and care needed to educate children with special needs should not apply.

Societal and peer-pressure effects on learning

Contemporary American society pulls young people away from school and toward social and recreational pursuits. Emphasis is placed on peer relations and maintaining a status quo that many times does not value education. Peer relations in inner-city schools place less of a premium on doing well in school, but place greater emphasis on having an active social life. The time of adolescence is when the student is striving to find an identity and acceptance, so the effect of peer pressure is strong.

In inner-city schools across the nation, students are not performing academically. The reason for this lack of focus as it relates to doing well in school has many variables that include environmental, familial, or peer group relations. These variables are external and therefore, the reasons for non-achievement are those of nurture.

Many irritated teachers are surrounded daily by students who refuse to utilize their full potential and who are headed for a less meaningful and difficult life. If there is any hope in motivating these students to succeed, it should be addressed, so that many social ills can be averted. Research yields many facts that should be taken into consideration: As many as approximately 30% of our youth drop out and fail to complete high school. The dropout rate of our nation's students is influenced by many factors, not just an unwillingness to learn. Many students have to leave school to take care of younger siblings or work to support their own offspring. Evidence supports the fact that most schools are not conducive to self-esteem since the level of self-esteem declines for most students the longer they are in school. This revelation may be due in part to the "factory model" of schooling that has been the structure of public education since the dawn of the industrial revolution. Students upon graduation are treated as products, ready to fit into the "societal cog" of work. If you think about it, children are grouped by age and are given the same lesson content step by step through each grade level as they were products going through the "assembly line". Another detriment to our society's educational status is the fact that many students do not see the benefit of getting a good education. In the past, the attainment of a diploma meant a certain qualification to enter the work force or to perform a trade for an established livelihood. In society today, the growing "knowledge economy ", the do it yourself attitude championed by expanded technologies, the existence of highly educated individuals who are unemployed, and the ever present status of many young celebrities in the fields of entertainment and sports have given students today a false sense of belief in the necessity of getting an education or graduating. Students may or may not believe in the benefits associated with getting a diploma, but to further add insult to injury is the fact that students are skeptical about the benefits associated with either learning or doing well in class. In other words, they believe that their success in the labor force will depend mainly on the number of years of schooling they complete if they finish at all, and not with learning what schools have to teach and being good at it.

Disruptive students and bullies as detriments to learning

The focus on why students with challenges fail to perform is warranted and much can be said, but let us look at the issue of those students who have a desire to do well but who are sidetracked and disrupted by the "bully" or "class clown." Why are all of the troublemakers allowed to stay in school longer than needed when their very presence can cause other students to imitate or change their behavior for the worst? There are many debates and perspectives on this issue and the fact that it is so difficult to resolve adds to the frustration of the irritated teacher. One perspective on the issue of troublemakers in school would be the idea to abandon the philosophy of every child getting an education. Of course this statement runs counter to the fiber of our collective American identity, What if we consider the option of "giving up" on the few? Although this perspective may appear to be mean and callous, what about the vast majority of children who want to learn? Should they be hindered by being in close proximity to those with no desire to learn? Keeping the kind and empathetic philosophy of not giving up on children may be depriving many children of and education they need and desire. What of the solution of setting up separate schools for the disruptive children to attend so that all the trouble makers are together bothering each other? Some think the strategy of kicking out all troublemakers will result in a bunch of troublemakers on the street with nothing to do during the day. This scenario is very feasible. This seems like inviting trouble. Others harbor the view that maybe it would help to stop viewing them as "troublemakers" and view them as kids who for some reason are inspired to sabotage their own life chances by causing trouble. Then we can somehow begin to get them some help and find out why they are causing trouble. Research in the human sciences has revealed that troublemakers are generally not happy or well-adjusted, and these individuals need to be addressed from this standpoint. Granted, the classroom where other kids want to learn about math or history may not be the best location to attempt to delve into psycho-social and environmental profiling, but this type of work must be done for those who oppose giving up on the troublemakers. Obvious limitations to this approach would be the priorities of the school system, funding, political priorities, etc. Giving up on troublemakers and expelling them or relegating them to a detention center or alternative school can solve the immediate problem of classroom disruption, but let us not forget possible ramifications of this approach. Universal education is based on the idea that society benefits from having a well-educated populace. If only educated people got jobs, then those without educations would be unemployed and unproductive. Another idea to keep in mind is the possibility that troublemakers will not stay that way their entire life. It is true that some trouble-making students grow up to become adults who function in society productively. The propensity for trouble is not a permanent condition, as many things that are done in childhood are extinguished as we mature. There are people who never out grow a disruptive personality, but thankfully, these types of individuals are outnumbered by those who do. The child who is sent to the principal's office in the fifth grade may turn out to be the president of the National Honor's society in the eleventh grade. Alternative education is where many bad-acting kids end up. I'm sure many success stories have come from alternative education, illustrating the value of educating at-risk people. It is a valid and noble opinion to educate trouble-makers and at risk children, but in the mainstream setting of a regular school, at risk students continue to cause irritation among teachers.

What about placing special needs students in regular classrooms, and holding teachers (without the adequate training) responsible for educating these children? Some people act out and cause trouble because they were abused or come from a bad home situation. Some people act up just because they have foul personalities. Many irritated citizens are in favor of splitting classes up into "tracks" by academic ability and effort. This also holds for not mainstreaming special needs children into regular classrooms. There are AP classes, there are general classes, and there are the low functioning classes. Of course, many people are against this kind of system because the underperformers might feel bad. As long as a student is willing to learn; then extra help and resources can be given. Whatever help is possible should be made available. If they have a legitimate learning disability, they should also receive special help from individuals who are trained in special education. Regular content area teachers who have no training in special education should not be tasked with teaching the type of student who has special needs. If a student is violent, dangerous, or otherwise continuously disruptive then they should be removed until they are ready to learn.

Standardized testing causes irritation in some educators

Another issue at hand is the fact that many public school teachers are forced to "teach to the test". Ubiquitous standardized testing does not provide educators the flexibility to teach in a manner that would be most beneficial to the educator or the student. Add to this scenario the ill-advised mainstreaming of physically and mentally disabled students into regular classroom populations. Teacher irritation is not only understood, but is expected. The education of all members of our society is crucial and those who have physical and mental challenges should not be excluded from learning all that they are able to acquire and process, however, students with these challenges need to receive specialized care that many educators are not equipped to give. Special education instructors and personnel are in-place to assist such students, and this assistance should be given in an exclusive environment. It is not wise to put these students in the same classroom as "normal" children who may or may not already have a desire to learn.

. Many standardized tests represent a broad consensus of what parents, classroom teachers, school administrators, academics, and business and community leaders believe schools should teach and students should learn. Many of the test focus on the four core areas of English, mathematics, science, and history/social science. A curriculum framework also is provided with many standardized tests that details the specific knowledge and skills students must possess to meet the standards for these subjects. The problem in many inner-city schools today is that students are not self-motivated, have little pride in their self-image, and allow their peers to negatively impact their academic performance. This low academic performance is also reflected in the low scores students receive on the standardized tests.

The federal mandate of No Child Left Behind has caused children with disabilities (both mental and physical) to be mainstreamed in "regular" classes with children who don't overtly demonstrate any physical, emotional, or information processing handicaps. Of course 'overtly" is the keys word, such that many students who are deemed normal have many of not all of the same issues as children who have been formally diagnosed and have subsequently been labeled. How is it even possible for teachers in our public schools, who are required to educate children from this demographic, to explain and reinforce content? Or better yet to get this demographic of children to apply content or pass standardized tests? What about the children who are classified as normal physically and mentally but because of hardships in their environment choose to disrupt class and choose to become behavior problems? If there is any hope in motivating these students to succeed, it should be addressed, so that many social ills can be averted. When people refuse to accept uncomfortable information, they get mad at the individual who attempts to show them. They "kill the messenger."

There are many educators who are at odds with the issue of standardized testing and "standardized answers". 'What is so wrong with standardized testing?" many of you may ask, let us analyze many of the cons of standardized testing that can cause some educators to become irritated.

In the interest of objectivity, it should be noted that standardized testing and standardized tests, in and of themselves are not bad things. Standardized testing is useful when diagnosing a problem or trying to determine if a student has learned what you've tried to teach them. It is when standardized test results are used as the major determining factor in making decisions regarding graduation, grade promotion, and funding. When standardized tests become high-stakes tests is when they become a problem. Arguments against standardized testing can be grouped into three larger arguments:

1. *High-stakes testing affects the curriculum being taught in schools, it affects how teachers teach their students, and usually affects how much meaningful learning takes place in a classroom.*
2. *High-stakes testing has huge negative impacts (as in emotional impact or material impact) on students, teachers, and schools.*
3. *Standardized testing becomes a problem when the test itself is biased against some of the students taking it.*

Each of these arguments has many subtle points which build to a greater argument. These points are addressed and explained further below. High-stakes testing affects the curriculum being taught in schools, it affects how teachers teach their students, and usually affects how much meaningful learning takes place in a classroom.

It is a common misconception that what is taught in the classroom and what is tested are the same things. Unfortunately, what students are tested on, don't always match up with the instructional content and objectives of the classroom. (Ormrod, 2002). When students are given a test, teachers often know beforehand what is going to be on that test or they have some kind of general idea of the concepts to be covered. They obviously want their students to do well, so they spend a lot of time covering those topics that are on the test. This is called "teaching to the test". This isn't so bad, but becomes a problem when teachers are forced to discard other topics they had planned on covering in order to spend more time on the concepts they know will be on the test. There is so much accountability for low test scores that teachers do everything in their power to raise them. They drill students on what they will be tested on and they go beyond the curriculum only to teach test-taking skills (Burley). When the curriculum is narrowed in such a fashion, students obviously lose out on a rich and full education. Some important facts can be gleaned from a discussion of standardized testing:

- *Most standardized tests are given as multiple choice tests. The focus on multiple choice testing limits teaching and learning to that of finding the "right answer" at the expense of skills and abilities such as critical thinking, creative thinking, and problem solving.*
- *A lot of school systems hold their schools accountable when test scores do not continually improve. They place an inordinate amount of pressure on teachers to raise students' test scores. Unfortunately, this can lead to dishonesty on the part of teachers and principals. They have no reason to include the scores of students with special needs and often try to find reasons why a student with special needs shouldn't even take the test (Ormrod, 2002).*
- *Results of high-stakes tests are often used to determine funding, salary increases and other administrative aspects. However, how do you determine which schools get what? Do they have to meet some standard of achievement, do they have to show continual improvement, or do they have to do better than all the other schools. Depending on which of these criteria you choose, you will reach different conclusions about which schools are performing well and which are not (Ormrod, 2002).*
- *Often times, after getting test results, we spend more time punishing schools and students that don't perform well. This punishment is done by federally taking over the school, and removing resources. Instead of spending that time helping*

those students and schools improve. Many times, schools cannot overcome long-standing poverty, racism, and neglect. Should they be punished? Is the scenario irritating?

- *One of the most devastating effects of high-stakes standardized testing is the emotional effects on students and teachers. After doing poorly on a test, low-achieving students become disillusioned and less motivated which leads to less effort to learn, starting a downward spiral that creates a negative emotion towards learning. Teachers have even admitted that they begin to develop negative attitudes towards students that do not perform at an acceptable level. Not only do the students get depressed after poor results on a standardized test, but teacher morale is lowered.*

- *One of the biggest faults of standardized tests is that they often do not take diversity into account. Too many of today's tests are written so that only white, middle-class, English-speaking Americans can succeed. Other aspects of diversity that tests often times don't take into account include:*

- ***Disabilities**-These include physical disabilities, language delays, ADHD, visual impairments, mental retardation, and the list could go on and on.*

- ***Test Anxiety**-It is not an uncommon thing for students to get debilitating test anxiety. Debilitating test anxiety does not refer to the butterflies in the stomach or that moment of panic when the test is passed out. Instead it refers to the students who may freeze and cannot perform at all when faced with a test.*

- ***Cultural Bias**-It is only common sense to assume that a test item including information specific to the American culture (as some items do on some standardized tests) will be harder to answer for a student not familiar with that part of American culture. Essentially a student is being penalized for not answering the question correctly even though they may know how to actually do the problem; they simply didn't understand the details given in the problem*

- ***Socioeconomic Status**-Standardized tests are also often biased against students from poorer socio-economic backgrounds. They may not have been exposed to these kinds* *of tests before or they may not be familiar with the aspects of a question. For example, a question asking about the nature of fresh-cut apples to brown in the presence of oxygen may be biased against a poorer student because their parents couldn't afford to buy a lot of fresh apples. Examples like these are extreme, but bias against students from different socio-economic backgrounds is a reality.*

Low funding for needed supplies causes irritation

Another issue that needs to be addressed that irritates many teachers is the lack of funding for supplies. We discussed earlier in the chapter entitled "the irritated citizen" the individuals who are in favor of cutting taxes. Cutting taxes means less money for all school programs including supplies. Aside from the teacher shortage, overcrowding of classrooms, cutting of arts and physical education classes, the national deficit and bad economy, teachers in many school districts are forced to pay for supplies out of their own personal funds. As funding is cut, so are the provisions that allow teachers to have the materials they need to deliver their content effectively. I have personally witnessed the irritation many teachers have expressed when they have to go to the store to buy paper, pens, glue sticks, etc. in order to have materials on hand when needed in class. The flip side of this equation also causes irritation in the teacher. The flip side is many parents choose not to supply their children with the necessities for school. This is not an attack against the parents who have no means to buy school supplies when the greatest portion of their income is used for the basic necessities of life (e.g. food, clothing, roof over the head, heat, water, electricity), nor is it an attack on the parents who are able and fulfill their roles, but it is an attack against those parents who are driven the possession of material items. Parents such as these spend money to make sure they or their children possess the nicest clothes and latest automobiles and gadgets; but they neglect the basic need of pencils and pens their child needs for class. Many times the student does not ask the parent for supplies, nor do they try to obtain the needed school supplies themselves. It amazes many educators that some children can have expensive sneakers, own the latest technological gadgets, get new hairdos weekly, but continuously walk into class without pencil or paper. If you are coming to school, why not have pencil and paper? In this instance, it is student and the parents who are to blame. While we are on the subject of funding, let us examine some of the issues that are relevant to this discussion. Given the fact that many teachers are irritated by their jobs, many are thankful to hold the position of an educator and feel that they can still contribute something of value to the generations of our nation. I want to stress the fact that the author knows many educators personally and they all appreciate their jobs. Many of them value the position the have to effect a change in developing minds, many enjoy the prestige and respect of being educators, and at a basic level, many are grateful to have a job that provides gainful income and does not fall victim to consumer desires or the marketplace.

Irritated with strategies aimed to decrease the need for teachers

Certain political ideologies seek to create a nation of unemployed teachers and unemployable citizens. What can be more irritating to an educator than a political structure set in place to cause him or her to lose their livelihoods? The irritated teacher is mad about individuals seeking to make the teaching profession obsolete.

American democracy is built upon public education. Public schools are failing and have numerous issues. We as a society are aware that many of these issues need to be solved and are for aggressive measures to accomplish resolution, but to abandon public education wholesale is not the answer. Many polls of the American people show that Americans would rather fix our schools that abandon them altogether (Earth Works Press, 2006).

Certain political viewpoints have supported the effort to undermine public education for years. Fundamentalist Christians for instance, believe that public education is poisoning the minds of their children with secular values and Anti-tax crusaders who want to privatize education are at the forefront of the push to shut down public education as we now know it (Earth Works Press, 2006).

It may be hard to accept that there are certain factions in America who want to do away with public education, but it is true.

Vast research shows the full scale strength of anti-public education initiatives. What many of these initiatives set out to do is dismantle federal and state control over public education and give control over to commercial and private interests. If schools are in private hands, you know what can happen: many families will not be able to afford education, there is a possibility of selective acceptance requirements, with the discrimination and exclusion of many students as the result, and most relevant to our present discussion, the cutting and loss of millions of teaching jobs across the nation. The ratio of teachers needed would decrease as hiring decisions would be made based on the number of families that can afford to pay for their children to attend school. For example, if only 20% of American families with school-aged children (5-18yrs.) can afford to send their children to school, then only 20% of all the qualified teachers who have had the requisite education and training will only be hired. In our present society, paying for a secondary education (e.g. college, grad school, law school, medical school) requires a substantial investment of money from all those involved. Advanced educations are a burden enough on families who may not be wealthy, but see the value of possessing higher educations, degrees, and certifications. Imagine having to finance a k-12 education that was once the right of every American individual to obtain, regardless of socio-economic status. That would be horrible.

The issue of No Child Left Behind was mentioned very briefly earlier in the book. We will examine the issue of No Child Left Behind and why it has caused irritation among many teachers. The No Child Left Behind Act was introduced in 2001 by the Bush administration and had bi-partisan support in Congress. Many believed the bill was created to improve public education, but in actuality the bill was created to undermine public education. The teacher's livelihood is once again put in jeopardy. Consider the argument presented in *50 ways to Fight the Right* by Earth Works Action, 2006:

> *If the idea is to improve schools, why is the act massively underfunded . . . and why are a majority of states unable to meet even the most minimal of its annual testing standards? In a study conducted in 2006, it was projected that 93% of Connecticut schools, 99% of California's,*

77% of Pennsylvania's, 75% of Massachusetts', 85% of Indiana's, 84% of Wisconsin's, 80% of Ohio's, 85% of Minnesota's, 85% of Illinois', and100% of Michigan's will be labeled failures, and that's only a partial list. In other words, over a 10 year period, practically every school in America would officially be considered a failure. And what would we have instead? Can you say "privatization?"(p. 105).

From being blamed for the failures of all the individuals who do not successfully complete their formal schooling, to not knowing if they will have a career in the next 10 years, it is understandable why many teachers are irritated with parents, students, and governments. The educator is irritated and upset because he or she is forced to motivate and educate students who see no value in learning. The teacher is forced to correct all of the wrongs that are represent in the young student's environment, and the teacher is not given freedom of technique or creativity in regards to delivering content because they have to teach to the test. As the reader, are you irritated with the teacher for "complaining" and not trying hard enough to teach our students content and life skills when many of their own parents and caregivers are unable to do so? Or are you irritated because the sad state of our education forces you to look into the mirror?

Irritated With Those Not Like Us: Limbic Resonance

5

D O YOU LOOK with contempt at people who choose to wear strange clothing or change the physical appearance of their bodies through piercing, scarring, tattoos or mutilation? Do you get irritated when you see interracial couples? Do you find yourself becoming upset when you see two people of the same gender holding hands or kissing? Do you hate it when others' don't see your point of view?

The world is diverse and it is natural and inevitable that we will run into situations where we are in proximity to people that are not like us. It is human nature to want to be around things that are familiar. It is also human nature to want to conform, to be accepted, or to be understood by others. Even in people who choose not to conform to the thoughts and actions of the majority, they often seek like minded groups to join that express the same anti-majority stance. Humans naturally prefer pleasure instead of displeasure. Traditional, mainstream beliefs are often more comfortable than deviant beliefs. A preference for comfort over discomfort is a basic psychological and physiological characteristic of sentient beings. It takes complex pathologies and motivations to choose displeasure. Many people who seek discomfort have either an agenda, a psychological disconnect, or a physiological illness. An individual's agenda is illustrated by that person's beliefs, and the assessment of another's beliefs is judged against on our personal preferences. Individuals who possess beliefs or behaviors that do not coincide with our personal beliefs fuel our irritation. We are irritated with those who are not like us.

Due to the fact that humans are ego-centric and view situations based on their personal biases and perceptions, humans tend to blame negative actions and behaviors on the "inferior" personality of others. In contrast, we tend to judge our own negative actions and behaviors on external causes rather than on our own personalities. For example, if someone is late to meet you, you tend to automatically consider the person to be rude or irresponsible. However, if you are the person running late to meet someone, you tend to blame your tardiness on circumstances such as traffic, the baby-sitter being late, bad directions, etc. These are examples of Fundamental Attribution Errors—which states that people will overemphasize personality-based causes, rather than situation based causes for the behaviors of others, but not for their own behavior. Because personality-based judgments are more typical when we analyze the behaviors of others, it is easy for us to blame the person and not blame the person's environment for their perceived deficits. This causes us to become irritated with individuals and not situations. This focus on the personality of others is what fuels our dislike of others that are different from us because we expect others to operate from the same "rational" mind-set we have. The environment is not a factor, because we feel subjectively we can overcome the environment and others should too. Threats to diversity can be thought of as any subjective or physical manifestation of thoughts or actions which can have a negative impact on an individual's sense of well-being. This sense of well-being can be threatened strictly on the basis of an individual's ethnicity, race, religion, gender, sexual orientation, or physical ability. Why do humans dislike those who are not like them? One way to analyze this human tendency is to look at the concept of limbic-resonance.

Limbic resonance and proximity as factors in group formation

The limbic system of the brain controls emotion and memory in humans. The limbic system can draw on the emotions of others until there is a simultaneous congruent emotion among people in close proximity. Limbic resonance is the term used to describe the congruent emotion. Limbic resonance is what makes it more fun, exciting, or sad to see a movie with others rather than alone. Limbic resonance is what can cause a crowd of individuals to become a hate-filled lynch mob or love-filled hippies wallowing in the mud at Woodstock. Limbic resonance, or the phenomenon of congruent emotions, can cause many in our society to become racists, homophobes, and religious fundamentalists with an overriding compulsion for violence. Our Limbic systems act as the antennae and the broadcaster of our emotional states.

The primordial brain in humans was created to fear what it does not understand. This fear of the unknown can be of perceived predators, imagined threats, or more specifically, those persons who have lifestyles and cultures we do not understand. An underlying theme of this book is existentialism, and existentialism forces some individuals to proclaim their presence in the world. The myriad ways individuals choose to proclaim their existence often irritate others. People may choose to express a deviant sexuality or choose to adopt a non-conformist lifestyle. Existentialism calls for an individual to create a meaningful existence in the world. A world that at times may seem meaningless. What should the individual live for? What path is the best way? Irritation with individuals is a result of the fact that humans organize their thoughts around reference groups. These reference groups of humans can be our families, our friends, our co-workers, individuals of a similar race or ethnicity, individuals who share similar sexual and religious orientations, and those who share propinquity with us.

Propinquity relates to the physical or psychological proximity between people. Propinquity can mean physical proximity, a kinship between people, or a similarity in nature between things. Two people with similar political beliefs possess a higher propinquity than those whose beliefs strongly differ. The propinquity effect is the tendency for people to form friendships or romantic relationships with those whom they encounter often. In other words, our reference groups are formed between those who have a high propinquity with us. While in close proximity to those in our reference group, our limbic systems take control. Our primordial brain reinforces its "survival instincts" and we formulate stereotypes of others whom we do not share a high propinquity. The stereotypes we form of others resonate strongly with others in our group; and when this occurs, threats to diversity and irritation with others is manifested.

Confirmation bias/ group polarization influences irritation with others

There are other theories similar in nature to limbic resonance; that help to explain why we come to dislike others why we become irritated with others. Two of these theories are *Confirmation Bias* and *Group Polarization*. As we have discussed earlier, individuals tend the form opinions of others based on the ideas of those in their reference groups and or those in close proximity. Confirmation Bias states that once a belief is set in place in the mind of the individual, that person will screen what they see and hear in a biased way that ensures their beliefs are proven correct. In other words, when we perceive new experiences, we tend to only focus on the aspects of that experience that validate what we already believe. Psychologists have also discovered that people are vulnerable to group polarization.

Group polarization is very similar to limbic resonance and occurs when people who share beliefs get together in groups. These groups become more convinced that their beliefs are correct and this leads to more extreme views and actions taken on by the members in the group. As a result, whole groups of people can become irritated, and as the group takes on a distinct mindset, the likelihood of *deindividuation* occurring amongst members is highly likely. Deindividuation is a concept in social psychology regarding the loosening of social norms in groups that have group polarization. For the purposes of this book, the effect of the group influencing the individual in terms of finding ideologies and people to be irritated with is analyzed. Theories of deindividuation propose that it is a psychological state of decreased morals and self-esteem within the individual that allows them to be so easily influenced by the group. With the decrease in moral judgment, comes an increase in maladaptive behavior. Deindividuation theory seeks to provide an explanation for a variety of maladaptive collective behavior, such as violence exhibited by crowds and lynch mobs. Deindividuation theory has also been provided as a possible theory for illegal and illicit behavior online and in computer-mediated communications. Deindividuation is a diminishing of one's sense of individuality that occurs when normal personal or social standards of conduct (morals) are diminished because the individual finds oneself the member of a larger group. In other words, someone who is an anonymous member of a group will be more likely to act violently or behave in ways not normal to the individual than if that person were alone and subject to personal evaluation and consequences. There is an obvious correlation between deindividuation and violent and antisocial behavior. It is the violent tendencies that are directed toward things we are irritated with that poses the greatest threat. The French psychologist Gustave Le Bon was an early researcher in deindividuation and he introduced his crowd psychology theory in his 1895 publication *The Crowd: A Study of the Popular Mind*. Le Bon characterized his posited effect of crowd mentality, whereby individual personalities become dominated by the collective mindset of the crowd. Le Bon theorized that a loss of personal responsibility in crowds leads to an inclination to behave primitively and hedonistically by the entire group.

All of this talk of deindividuation leads one to question whether many of our irritations are based on our own personal interpretations, or whether they are the result of other people's attitudes? Some of our irritation with those not like us can be attributed to the fact that we have been made a victim of deindividuation by our simple desire to belong to a group. We don't like those persons who have enough individuality to not belong because it subconsciously makes us feel inferior because we realize we do not possess the strength of character to not seek approval from others. Those who are not like us may cause us to become irritated not because they have caused us harm or have the ability to threaten us; it may simply be because they choose not to subscribe to our "reference group polarization". This makes us irritated.

Irritated with the Media

6

A man is likely to mind his own business when it is worth minding. When it is not, he takes his mind off his own meaningless affairs by minding other people's business. This minding of other people's business expresses itself in gossip, snooping, and meddling, and also in feverish interest in communal, national and racial affairs. In running away from ourselves we wither fall on our neighbor's shoulder or fly at his

—Eric Hoffer—*The True Believer*

IT IS A fact that the First Amendment of the United States Constitution protects the public's right to know. This right to know is the basis for all media that seek to inform. In contemporary society the development of technology,, especially electronic media allows for an increasing exposure to multiple viewpoints. As a result of the readily available nature of differing viewpoints to any number of issues or events, the belief in any one objective reality does not exist. Media also serves the function of entertainment. In the quest of providing knowledge and entertainment to our society, do the media use the wrong methods? More importantly, are you unhappy with the types of news stories that are constantly broadcast? Do you wonder why the majority of news stories involve crime, death, celebrities, or lawlessness? Do you find yourself depressed by simply picking up the news paper or watching your local news or CNN? Do you have a credit rating less than satisfactory and your debt increasing due to constant advertising for newer and better material items you really do not need? Do you feel deep down in your gut that there has to be other types of human activity going on in all parts of the world that is not negative? Let us examine the media and why it has the tendency to make us frustrated.

News events are chosen to serve specific needs in society

Of the millions of events that take place in the world on any given day, only a tiny percentage of the events are made into news. Let's face it, even with our advanced technology, it would be difficult to get every event that ever occurs to a mass audience is a coherent format. After all, we are not even able to record, capture or disseminate all the events that happen on a daily basis in our own homes. This fact presents the necessity of "choosing" which events to disseminate. Stories that are typically selected for media coverage are stories that confirm the viewpoint of the dominant culture. The dominant culture has to power to define what is deviant and what is newsworthy. Events that disconfirm the dominant cultural viewpoint are ignored or given little attention. This function of the media reinforces the irritation we subconsciously feel toward "those that are not like us" discussed elsewhere in the book. The paradox is of course, stories that are given little attention in the media of one culture; may be front news in the media of another. This statement carries extreme importance as advances in technology allow many cultures and viewpoints to have a public ear. The major factor is the strength and amount of human exposure the particular mode of media can attract. For even though one culture may deem important an idea that is neglected by another culture, which culture (while presenting their viewpoint) reaches the greatest audience? Given that the audience can be dependent on the wealth, technology, and population of the parent culture. This phenomenon is intensified when there is conflict between cultures. In the scenario when the same event is covered by differing cultures, it is conceptualized very differently. A great example of this difference of conceptualization would be the reporting of news stories involving war. During wartime, each side tells the story of the conflict to its home audience in self-serving terms. Although both sides commit atrocities, each side's media will only highlight the atrocities of its enemy, while suppressing and minimizing its own brutalities. It is an established fact that the mass media has a self-serving function. As stated by Jerome Frank:

It seems that stories that get the most exposure are capable of negatively affecting the mind-sets of the target culture or audience. This is the gripe being presented here. The media outlets of our culture (United States of America) present news stories which foster certain agendas, scare us, stress us, and cause us to become conspicuous consumers

There is no doubt that the media outlet of television serves a major role in the lives of many Americans. Television not only provides entertainment and information, but television drives our desires, feeds our subconscious (more on this later), and creates our reality. According to Postman (2005):

Individuals today live in a different media environment than in the past, as a result our relationship to television has changed. In today's society, many individuals have choices of over 900 channels that speak to every interest of those in our population. In today's society, television is a 24 hour endeavor (p.).

Research has been documented that shows on average, Americans spend more than 40 percent of their free time watching television. Research also shows that on average, televisions in most homes in America are turned on for longer than seven hours a day. Add to this the internet and there is little doubt that the media has a great influence of the daily lives of many individuals. Individuals utilize the media to surf the net, to be entertained, to relax, to escape, to avoid loneliness, and to gain information. One major way people gain information through television or the internet is through the news. Humans in our present day societies want news that requires only small bites, is easily digested, and can be absorbed quickly. Could this preference for quick and simple presentation reflect the greater population's preference for fast food and instant gratification? As the nuggets of information have become smaller and the chunks of entertainment have become larger, the amount of information that the internet and television provides and the way in which it is provided have changed (think of the "ticker tape" presentation of news bites at the bottom of the screen on many national and local news broadcasts). According to Day (1996) there is also a trend toward the "Hollywoodization" of the news. This euphemism has been coined by CBS Evening News anchor Dan Rather. The "Hollywoodization" of the news, is when there is greater interest in the personalities, celebrities, and environments of the news item than in the substance.

"Trash" television masquerading as serious news or serious information

The proliferation of news with no substance has led to what can be termed "tabloid television". You have talk shows such as *Maury* and *Jerry Springer* whose very existence on television is to both create and perpetuate a specific audience that craves uncouth media. On these talk shows, the guests cover a wide range of subjects that gravitate toward, sex, adultery, violence, and ignorance.

Because of the ubiquitous nature of television in society, an alternate reality is created which structures our perceptions. A specific negative attribute of this phenomenon can be said to be how stereotypical views are constructed and maintained by television.

One major aspect that needs to be addressed is the advent of reality television. Reality television provides limited interpretations of factors involved in the real situation. Unlike documentaries which tend to be more academic and show the good and the bad sides of the given idea, reality-based shows generally air only the good or the bad and fail to show both sides. Police officers always use correct tactics and judgment and emergency personnel never make mistakes. Some critics say this is not by accident. Producers of reality based programs rely on the cooperation of the public agencies involved. If their operations were shown negatively, the agencies would cut off access to the producers and there would be no program. The editing for many of these shows involves deleting out unflattering scenes and editing in dramatic scenes. Producers often allow the agencies to have a say in what is shown. The result is that viewers don't get the complete story.

Take for example the show "Survivor". Everyone is aware of the day-to-Day trials and tribulations of the contestants while on the island, but once they are sent home, then what? The media may request the "survivor" contestant to do an interview on a morning show such as "Today" or maybe on a commercial. Other than any number of quests spots or movie appearances this person may have, what is followed up regarding the changes to that person's personal life? Did that individual lose his or her job as a result of being away on television for weeks? What was the impact on that individual's family life (children or spouse)? Did the individual lose friends due to jealousy? These are the various after-effects of reality that these "mini-celebrities" are faced with when they return home. The unpleasant consequences of life are often "cleaned-up" or disregarded as they are not entertainment.

Another way television creates reality is the proliferation of channels broadcasting real phenomena on a continuous basis. An example of this would be the Weather Channel. According to Postman *"while dissemination of weather information is needed, the Weather Channel has also shown numerous shows on tornadoes and try to make the weather seem fun."* Broadcasting natural disasters as entertainment cleans up reality and makes us desensitized. An alternate reality is created.

The manufacturing of paranoia is irritating.

Our present society is an information society. As such, the availability of information, especially news, via ever changing and sophisticated technologies have created a population that is paranoid, stressed, and unable to accurately judge truth and reality. This manufacturing of paranoia is what is irritating.

George Gerbner, who was the director of the Annenberg School of Communications at the University of Pennsylvania circa 1996, has studied heavy television viewers. Heavy television viewers can be defined as those who watch six or more hours of television a day. These heavy viewers have what Gerbner calls the *"mean world syndrome."* The mean world syndrome is characterized by feelings of danger, mistrust, intolerance, gloom, and hopelessness. People with mean world syndrome grossly overestimate the incidence of crime and violence in the world. An acquaintance of mine one stated "Nothing is exciting about doing the right thing." A study by the

Annenberg's Survey Research Center showed that of people who are heavy television viewers, almost 25 in every 100 say there is a very serious chance that they will be victimized, while only 6 in every 100 light television viewers feel that way. The media have also been accused of exaggerating dangers to scare the public. In the past, a Florida man filed suit alleging that a cellular phone caused his wife's fatal brain tumor. The media played up the possible risks of cell phone use. Often the press can be just as scientifically illiterate as the general public. Journalists can misuse statistics, misunderstand the scientific process, and mistake prudence for alarm. "The Media are in the outrage business" states a consultant who advises companies about risk. The media fuels its stories and information with a bias towards controversy and emotion. Most television newscasts will include powerful sound bites that invariably reflect the outer extremes of the issue. This practice reinforces the impression of society as highly polarized and squeezes out the middle ground or moderate perspective. News networks such as Fox, CNN, MSNBC and others create an alternate reality that does not allow the individual to think critically or realistically about events that are taking place in the immediate environment. I often wonder about the kind of life that was led by an aware, intelligent, contributing adult of the 1950's and 1960's. I use these time frames as I reflect on the youth of my grandmother (81 years old as I write this) and would have been 20-30 years of age during the 50's and 60's. Surely tasked with worrying over the assumed responsibilities of their families and survival (just as other families during that time was as well as today) did my grandparents or other adults during that time period exhibit the same paranoia over news that did not occur directly in their immediate communities? My theory is that they did not. Adults of the past were not aware of such news mainly because technology had not advanced to the degree that each and every individual can see and hear (much less read) about news 24 hours a day from all over the globe. Death and natural disasters are newsworthy events of course, but hearing about these unfortunate events all day long everyday seems to me to serve no other purpose than to make people scared and angry at the expense of providing information. Do these stressful feelings help people interact with each other day-to-day in positive ways? My theory is that they do not.

George Lakoff in *The Political Brain* states that *"stresses like fear (of terrorist attacks), worry (about finances), health care, and so on), and overwork tend to activate the norephinephrine system, the system of negative emotion."* What good is it for the individual to walk around with negative emotions triggered by wired brain chemicals on a continuous basis? It is obvious that the production of norephinephrine occurs continuously because news outlets are available continuously via internet, 24 hour news networks, and newspapers. How can the individual not develop stress related illnesses? Does the individual have the mental energy to discern what is accurate and most useful in order to better his or her situation in this life? When the brain is experiencing an overload of negative neurotransmitters, the brain has a reduced capacity to reason objectively. This again illustrates the point of the book that our perceptions sometimes cause us to not see things objectively. According to Baines (1995):

> *The press and radio constantly bombard the individual with disconcerting news from all parts of the world. In ancient times, most of the events that took place daily were ignored and communications took months or even years to reach their destination. Unfortunately, today there is an informational atmosphere that is markedly morbid in which basically only those tumultuous events in which there is bloodshed or which are of an alarming nature qualify as "news". This has transformed the mentality of the great mass to such a degree that it seeks precisely the type of morbid information that arouses the imagination and it ignores news of positive events. The natural result of this type of information in the individual, is a subconscious state of anxiety which becomes chronic over time. Alarming news of wars in certain parts if the world and of the prospects of world war make on live in an inner climate of anxiety. Each individual has the "sword of Damocles" hanging over his head"*

The media as an agent of propaganda

James Hall in *Practically Profound* presents the idea that people prefer certain beliefs because they are familiar. If people did not generally prefer familiar beliefs over unfamiliar ones, there would be no need for advertising. The chief goal of advertising is to brainwash society by making certain products and ideologies so familiar that they become fixed points of reference in the common thought process of a society. This "brainwashing" is called propaganda. Propaganda can be thought of as the manufacture of mass consent or dissent. Propaganda will always work even as the world becomes more sophisticated and intelligent, as long as the propaganda appears true and is social in nature. Psychologists state that many of an individual's thoughts and actions are manifested to compensate for other desires that are repressed because the individual is ashamed of the true desire. It is the issue of desire that is relevant here. The desires of the population are what drive the media which in turn can cause irritation in many of us.

Are you sometimes made upset by the constant commercials, the constant claims, and the constant invitations to indoctrination that pop up on your computer, interrupt your favorite programs on television, or run daily via news/political television? Irritation with the media is what occurs if you are in fact made upset by the above questions. Baines (1995) writes:

> *The individual is continuously and repeatedly bombarded by commercial publicity which infiltrates his privacy and attempts to control his mind, and directs his preferences towards specific goods or services. As the assaults on an individual's consciousness are varied and numerous, the assaults create profound conflicts n the subconscious mind and of course bring on a state of tension*

Media as a contributor to violence in society is irritating

It is this tension that creates irritation. Does the ubiquitous nature of violence and sex on the internet and 24 hour television contribute to the de-sensitization of individuals and a disregard for human life?

This question can be said to originate from images circulated by the media. Although a direct cause and effect with regard to exposure to sex and violence and its effect is hard to establish, a definite correlation exists. The proliferation of negative images in the media may be a reason why people are more likely to kill others as well as themselves when they are upset or distraught. Mainstream media allows for instant celebrity and recognition, so that in some cases it may be that the individual has a death wish, but wants to take others with them to increase notoriety while killing him or herself. This is just a tentative stab at a possible motivation for a small amount of persons, but it is plausible nevertheless.

Being informed is a good thing, but is so good at the risk of becoming depressed or afraid to venture out into public? Is it so good that you disregard your own daily struggle and the daily struggles of others just to idolize over celebrities who don't even know you exist, nor care that you do? Are you irritated with others who constantly want to discuss the latest celebrity or murder, when you have more positive, self-improvement concerns on your mind? Are you irritated because the conversation with this person will make your mood sour, or are you irritated because this person refuses to believe the lies they have witnessed via the news broadcast and you do believe the lies?

Irritated With Having Something to Prove

7

*"You judge yourself by what you think you can achieve,
others judge you by what you have achieved"*

—Confucius

A RE YOU AN individual who tires of having to "keep up with the Joneses" The humanist psychologist Carl Rodgers states that people develop a need for positive regard that reflects the desire to be loved and respected. Because others provide this positive regard, we grow dependent on their interaction and assessment of us. This chapter speaks to intrinsic and extrinsic motivation. Motivation can be defined as—the factors that direct and energize the behavior of humans. Incentive approaches to motivations suggest that we are motivated by desires evoked by our internal environments. Cognitive approaches to motivation suggest that we are motivated by our thoughts and feelings. Which approach do you more heavily rely upon when you are motivated to do something? In the context of the cognitive approach, we may be drawn to a behavior that is its own reward, e.g. (reading or sleeping). These are *intrinsic motivations.* In other cases, when we are drawn to activities that promise rewards like money, a new car, or social approval, these are *extrinsic motivations*. Let's look at an example of how intrinsic and extrinsic motivations work together. The example given is sex. The sex drive is related to pleasure fulfillment on a physical level, but it also plays a crucial role in the survival of our species. Since the sex drive is important to both the individual and the entire human race, we can assume that many of our other motivations also benefit the individual and society. Social approval includes individual incentives, and at the same time, group incentives. Take for example the baseball player who is motivated to try and hit a home-run. The ball player has intrinsic motivations of wanting to feel successful and useful to the team, and at the same time, the team has a go of winning the game. If the ball player is able to hit the home run, the individual feeds his intrinsic motivation and his extrinsic motivation. The extrinsic motivations can be the reward of money (in the case of professional athletes) or being selected to the all-star team. The group benefits because the run scored from the home-run places the team in a closer position to winning the game. The benefits of group incentives are what fuel the strength of limbic resonance and group polarization discussed earlier in the book.

Psychological need for achievement

Social psychologist David McClelland has been recognized as a major contributor of ideas about achievement needs. His studies are important because they are based on careful and exhaustive research that spans a number of years. McClelland proposed that we could measure what he called *"the need for achievement"*. The need for achievement is the desire to meet or exceed personal standards. In general, people who are willing to take risks, have a high sense of their own ability, and have a drive to succeed are likely to be achievers and thus have the "need for achievement". Strongly correlated with the need to achieve is the need for affiliation and power. Many people are motivated by power and the feeling of belonging. The people who have the need to belong are the people who are relevant to our discussion. The affiliation need is high in people who strive for social acceptance or who derive satisfaction from social relationships. Again, this need for affiliation drives the irritation people experience with regards to others "who are not like us".

Extrinsic and intrinsic motivations can also be explained existentially. The ideas of Hegel help to explain motivation from the existentialist orientation. Hegel's idea that is relevant to our work is his "struggle for recognition. For Hegel, self-consciousness is the awareness of oneself as being aware. This is one of the qualities that make human beings different from other living beings. Hegel asserts that self-consciousness becomes certain of itself only through the struggle for recognition. There is only one way an individual's self-conscious can prove itself, that way is through the verification of another person. The individual is recognized for what he or she claims to be by the acceptance of that claim by another individual. The impulse toward self-consciousness ought to be determined solely by the individual. Why must the struggle for recognition be a constant struggle? Since my demand for recognition is based on how you recognize me as a self-conscious being, it must be determined that I am seen and recognized as purely self-determining. Nothing and no one can dictate to me. For this statement to be true, I must be able to eliminate, or dominate, anyone or any situation that threatens my self-determination and my control over my situation. In relation to you, from whom I demand recognition, I can only become self-determining if I can impose my terms on you. If you are in a position to influence the condition of my existence, then I will not be fully self-determining in the way I need to be. In the struggle for recognition, the death of one of the contenders would represent a loss for the victor. If the antagonist is actually killed, then the crucial goal of the winner, which is recognition, is not attained. His opponent is no longer able to provide recognition since he no longer exists. Unfortunately, the only satisfactory resolution of the struggle is domination of the vanquished by the victor. This is why Hegel asserts that the struggle for recognition must be comparable to the relationship of the master and slave. It is a sad fact that liberation can't come from simply refusing the struggle for recognition. This is the reason why the act of promoting ourselves to gain recognition by others (or having something to prove) causes irritation. Refusing to seek recognition from our peers can easily become a self defeating attitude that rejects the world altogether. The attempt to "opt out" of the struggle for recognition becomes socially suicidal. So the individual chooses to participate in the never ending cycle of striving for recognition and proving themselves to others,

The collective pursuit of immediate gratification is irritating

Our society is in a pathetic struggle to pursue immediate gratification. This quest for immediate gratification has no regard for the past or the future. The instant fulfillment of every transient whim, lust, or greed is desirable. This desirable urgency fuels a need to validate our individuality in the eyes of our reference groups. When we feel we have not been validated by those in our reference group, or that others have not recognized our accomplishments, or feel the sting when others ask us what we will do in the future, we become exhausted and irritated. According to John Baines:

> *Each day throughout the world, thousands of books are published on the subjects of new techniques and new knowledge. The enormous cultural machinery created by the human being threatens to engulf him, or at least drive him mad. There is no relationship between the velocity of cultural advance and the human capacity for learning. This velocity of change has caused an uncontrollable state of collective anguish and distress*

Exhaustion as a cause of irritation

In addition to anguish and distress over constantly trying to validate our existence in the eyes of others, is the inevitability of mental exhaustion. It is my opinion that exhaustion breeds irritation. The exhaustion I am referring to is the daily struggle for survival, the daily struggle to find one's purpose, the daily struggle of gaining social acceptance, and the daily struggle to meet our personal desires. The whole of these struggles are overwhelming. Relationships are needed between humans in order to fulfill biological and psychological necessities. Many evolutionary psychologists and biologists believe that our species would not have survived without a cooperative social instinct. Group cooperation and cohesion was essential to fight of attacks from wild animals. Man is a social being and as such needs to have relationships with others of his species. Irritation creeps in when the individual feels he or she has to constantly behave in socially acceptable ways or has to possess certain attributes whether materially or personally. The individual often feels that no matter what they have accomplished or done in the past, there is another "test" to conquer in the future just to appear acceptable to one's reference group. The striving for acceptance within one's reference group can easily be examined in an individual's spending on material items. Spending is a comparative activity. Desire is based on what we see around us (this is the basis of advertising), but in terms of one's social relationships, people look for validation (recognition) from those is a particular social space. For most of us this particular social space is our reference group. Our reference group begins with friends, relatives, and co-workers. They are the people against whom we judge our own material lifestyles. They are the groups that spur our consumer desires. When our consumer desires are activated, we spend more. It is the feeling of "my best is not good enough, and I still have to keep on proving myself until I die". This situation is similar to the situation I feel occurs with those who have material riches. The individual who is able to buy many things has the added responsibility of maintenance and up keep of those new items. This phenomenon can be called the "Diderot Effect". The Diderot Effects states that striving for conformity forces individuals to purchase new items that have to go along with the items just newly obtained. For example, if you purchase the newest cell phone out, it is very probable that you would consider purchasing the new memory card and applications that are available for that phone. Further, if you buy new china for your dining room, of course the Diderot effect makes you want to get new glassware and silverware to compliment it. Imagine if you had to means and desire to purchase a fleet of 15 new, classic, and antique automobiles. After purchasing these cars, where will they be stored? Who will maintain these vehicles to keep them in pristine condition? For these vehicles, mechanics will have to be employed, storage facilities and security systems purchased, as well as the added stress of insurance and paperwork for each of the vehicles. A less dramatic example would be the purchasing of video game system. With the purchase of this new item are the added costs of games that are not compatible with the old system you had, and the constant onslaught of newer accessories to outfit your system. The point I am making with these two examples is that when you acquire new circumstances, whether materially, personally, or professionally, new demands and pressures are added that you have to negotiate in order to exist successfully within the domain of your new life context. As the saying goes from an old rap song 'more money. More problems". At this point it is important to note that not all individuals stress over concerns of appearing successful, being a role model, or being a provider. Some individuals, due to life circumstances and personal beliefs, have very limited social networks. Individuals such as this may further feel no need in trying to adjust to what others would have them be and could not care less if they are not viewed as successful of personable. Individuals such as this are not irritated by the constant demands of social acceptance and reference group admiration.

The famous humanist-based psychologist Abraham Maslow developed the idea of self-actualization. It is my opinion that when the biological goals of the hierarchy of needs are met, then the individual begins the quest for peer acceptance and social efficacy. Propinquity and peer group acceptance are major factors in the constant game of proving ourselves to others that we find ourselves in. The question we ask ourselves is this: what have we done lately? Often this question is asked by family, friends, and associates on the job or at the church. This is where the stress and frustration can set-in. Many of us "wear masks" to fit into the differing roles we are expected to play in the course of our everyday interactions with others, whether personal or private. A poem written by the poet E. Jones examines the stress and irritation that is caused by having something to prove to others:

The Masks We Wear
By: E. Jones(2008)

Interchangeable and deceptive
Reflective of only the moments during which it's worn
for its purpose
We wear masks so the surface of what's hidden will
never be revealed
But forbidden to be viewed by anyone other than you
Each mask is natural and unique; Adjustable,
depending on how you
Speak into existence the mask's ultimate task
We bask in the joy of knowing creativity is infinite when
constructing our masks
Because whichever impression is first displayed is the
one which will last

*Until another mask is the centerpiece for our personal
exhibition
By masking our souls, we exhibit an untrustworthy
nature
That's been around since the beginning of time
We would assume since our climb from primeval
practices, the tactical moments
Of mask preparation would act as gifts for ingenuity,
but no, more masks occupy
the viewing scene for you and me condoning the
truancy of openness and trust
Our masks lust to be worn, so redevelopment and
overhaul above all
Dominated the mind which leaves no time for
consideration or contemplation
Of becoming free to show, grow and unfold our true
souls that are tucked away
Only to be masked by insecurity; Do our masks hide
impurities?
For some it may, but most masks come into play
because
from day to day the desired mood changes
We never tire from wearing the face, but a mask
remains handy just in case
Our souls ever become . . . revealed*

The fact must be pointed out that many individuals are not
concerned with the notion of social acceptance or appearances,
so they do not suffer the irritation of trying to live up to and meet
constantly changing standards, both personally or peer-group
imposed.

Irritated with Every Driver on the Road

8

"Traffic was as much an emotional problem as it was a physical and mechanical one."

—Henry Barnes

THE BOTTOM LINE is this; we all want the road for ourselves. Are you an irritated driver who gets road rage easily? If you are, then join the author and many others in what has become one of the greatest sources of stress and irritation. Many of us take driving as a simple endeavor. But it is actually an incredibly complex and demanding task. When we drive, we are navigating through a legal system, we are social participants in a spontaneous setting, and we are processing a great deal of information (making predictions and on-the-spot decisions), and we are engaging in a huge amount of sensory and cognitive activities (Vanderbilt 2008).

It has been stated that we spend more time in traffic than we do eating meals with our family or having sex. Our society is said, to spend more money on driving (car purchase, maintenance, insurance, gas, tags, etc.) than we spend on food or healthcare. It is paradoxical that the thing we do very often causes us some of the greatest amounts of irritation. It is paradoxical that the thing we spend the most money on (aside from housing) causes us some of the greatest amounts of irritation. Vanderbilt (2008) states:

> *Traffic has become a way of life. The expanding car cup holder, which became fully realized standard equipment only in the 1980s, is now the vital enabler of dashboard dining, a "food and beverage venue" hosting such*

products as Campbell's Soup at Hand and Yoplait's Go-Gurt. In 2001, there were 134 food products that featured the word go on the label or in ads; by 2004, there were 504. Accordingly, the number of what the industry calls "on-the-go eating occasions" in the United States and Europe combined is predicted to rise from 73.2 billion in 2003 to 84.4 billion in 2008. Fast-food restaurants now clock as much as 70 percent of their sales at drive-through windows. (Early in our romance with the car, we used to go to "drive-in" restaurants, but those now seem relics of a gentler, slower age.) An estimated 22 percent of all restaurant meals are ordered through a car window in America, but other places, like Northern Ireland-where one in eight people are said to eat in the car at least once per week-are getting into the act too. McDonald's has added a second lane to hundreds of its restaurants in the United States in order to speed traffic, and its new drive-throughs in China, dubbed De Lai Su (for Come and Get it Fast"), the company is pitching retooled regional offerings like rice burgers" to its burgeoning drive-through customers. Starbucks, which initially resisted the drive-through for its fast food connotations, now has drive-throughs at more than half of its new company-owned stores. The "third place" that Starbucks espouses, the place for community and leisure between home and work, is arguably the car" (p. 16).

Why does an activity that many of us engage in and depend on daily cause us so much frustration? Do you find your blood boiling when people drive faster than you as if your car is somehow inferior or the current rate of speed that you are travelling is hindering their "extremely important lives?" Do you get irritated when stuck in traffic when you know you should have left 45 min earlier? Do you get man when cars cut in front of you and slow down, better yet, do you get mad when another car cuts in front of you and is not going slower, but is driving faster or maintaining and adequate momentum? The irritation you feel about the aforementioned scenario is a result of being angry at having someone in front of you disturbing your previous field of vision. The bottom line of why we get irritated with other drivers is this: we each want the road for ourselves so we can have the freedom to come and go as we please and not have to be reminded of the selfishness of others exhibited by their choice of car and driving styles on the road. The actual manifestation of our irritation when driving is *road rage*. Road rage can be linked to our personal sense of what is right. According to Vanderbilt (2008) while driving, we obey a complex system of regulations, but the road is a place where many millions of people from different walks of life, ages, races, classes, ideologies, and religions mingle freely together on our nation's roads.

Our needs not being acknowledged on the road is irritating

On a personal level, what irritates me most about other drivers is my perception that they feel that their time and desires are more important than my own. When cars speed around me, constantly switch lanes while doing 80mph or greater, or make unsafe, illegal turns in the middle of the street, I become irritated. What is going on in the life of these drivers at that moment that they feel that their time and circumstances are so much more important than others on the road? We all share the road, so why should they put other lives in danger by making illegal turns in the road just because they feel they want to go another direction at the spur of the moment? Why should they put other lives in danger just because they feel they want to go faster than the car next to them? Drivers that irritate us are the ultimate manifestations of selfishness. Selfishness in our perceptions and attitudes and what causes us to become irritated as a result of those perceptions and attitudes is the theme of this book.

Possible reasons for road rage

Let's look at some of the possible psychological reasons why we get road rage. One such explanation according to Feldman (2010) is the *Frustration-Aggression Theory*. The Frustration-Aggression Theory suggests that frustration (the reaction to the thwarting or blocking of goals) produces anger. When we as humans internalize our anger, we look for cues in the environment that will allow us to act aggressively. This release of aggression works on the presence of *aggression cues.* Driving is the aggression cue for many people.

Driving can be a dangerous endeavor, and even when our personal safety is not threatened, we become anxious and irritated. We as drivers become obsessed with "teaching a lesson" to the offending driver of the other car. Tailgating illustrates this behavior. As we strive to "pay-back' another driver with the same irritation and frustration we have experienced, drivers also possess the constant desire to gain a personal advantage while behind the wheel. This quest to gain an advantage is our human selfishness if full effect.

Asymmetry of communicative interaction as a reason for irritation

There are other explanations given to why we experience road rage. One such explanation that is commonly given is that something upsetting happened to the driver prior to him or her taking the wheel. A car is a machine, and given this fact, drivers have limited means to communicate or express their frustrations in response to the driving of others. This phenomenon is called *asymmetry of communicative interaction.* According to Katz (1999):

"Whether stuck in traffic or watching cars freely speed by, each driver has reason to sense that his or her own vivid awareness of other cars is not reciprocated" (p.26).

Irritated drivers search the environment constantly to find a way of forcing other drivers to acknowledge their existence (this is one reason why many people choose to customize their cars). Katz goes on to state findings from his research (1999):

> *I have reviewed a few ways that drivers, when becoming angry on the road, acknowledge the expressive limitations of their vehicles in the actions they take to overcome them ... What drivers get mad about is their own dumbness, experienced as a sensed inability to get other drivers to take them into account. An emphatic instance was provided by Phillip, a twenty-five-year-old rock band musician. He reported that when he is behind someone who is driving*

> *slowly and who does not pull over so that he can pass, he*
> *will at times get in front of the person and slow down, to*
> *say 'you fucking see me now, bitch!'"*(p. 28).

The point to be made here is that the perception by the driver of not being able to fully articulate thoughts and frustrations, and of not having their presence validated by other drivers is a prime motivator for being irritated while driving.

My car represents my physical body while on the road

It is important we look at another aspect of being irritated with every driver on the road and that is the idea that the car is an outgrowth of our physical body. If you think about it, passengers typically do not have the same emotional experience as the driver. Based on this, it follows that passengers rarely experience or express road rage to the degree that the driver does. According to Katz (1999):

> *Sitting next to a driver, a passenger may observe the same*
> *rudeness, feel frustrated by the same traffic, be startled by*
> *the same aggressive conduct on the part of other drivers,*
> *but watch with amusement or fear as the driver of his or*
> *own car gets mad*(p. 31).

There seems to be crucial difference between the orientation of the passenger and that of the driver (Katz, 1999). The difference lies in the fact that the driver, in order to manipulate and operate the car effectively, must be embodied by the car. The car becomes the mechanical extension of the driver's body. To get "cut off" by another driver, for instance, is an accurate metaphor. It literally expresses the feeling that part of the driver's body has been cut off.

Thus far, we have discussed possible explanations for why people may develop road rage. It is important to keep in mind that when many of us as drivers witness someone expressing road rage towards us (and in some instances expressing road rage towards others), we in turn become irritated. Our thought processes based on the stimuli of witnessing or being the intended target of road rage, adds fuel to the fire and the cycle continues.

Like most people who experience first-hand the chaos of rushing around in traffic and dealing with aggressive drivers, any discussion that concerns road rage is sure to trigger emotional responses. When we think of aggressive driving, we think of actions such as: speeding, tailgating, weaving recklessly through traffic, ignoring stop signs and red lights, and cutting off other drivers. These signs of aggression can progress to great extremes and causes our irritation.

Road rage is more pervasive than one can imagine. Dr. John A. Larson, author of *Steering Clear of Highway Madness*, groups aggressive drivers into five categories:

- *Speeders*
- *passive aggressors*
- *narcissists*
- *vigilantes*
- *competitors*

Several characteristics are related to the most typical aggressive driver: being under 35, single, no education and a mid-level income. Furthermore, although women are more likely to confess to angry driving, men are more likely to participate in true "road rage", in which an angry driver intentionally harms another driver. Whether or not an aggressive driver takes physical action depends on the degree of anger he or she feels. "If someone pulls out in front of you or cuts you off, you may be justified at four or five on a scale of 10 . . . if you're up to seven to 10, though, that's an exaggerated response," says Larson.

Redford Williams, M.D., at Duke University, points to a hostile personality type as an indicator of someone who is more likely to get angry quicker. "They are also four to seven times more likely to die of other health problems by age 50 than are more even-tempered people," said Williams. For example, people with long drives to work are found to have higher blood pressure than people who take shorter routes to work. One frustrated commuter states, "it feels unnatural to forget about the jerk riding my tail or ducking in front of me to save half a second and some drivers—not me, of course—respond to overaggressive road behavior as if piloting a car were a contest. They drive to 'win' rather than simply to get to their destination."

In a nationwide poll of 1,100 licensed drivers, conducted July29 through Aug. 5, 2004, results show that 21—to 24-year-olds are most likely to be fast and aggressive drivers. The poll has a margin of error of plus or minus 3 percentage points. Generally, the actions that usually push motorists to the limit are failure to use turn signals, not paying attention, blocking a passing lane and tailgating, according to the American Automobile Association. Women and men, however, have different views. One in four men admits to driving angry, compared to one in five women.

Women seem to be more bothered by aggressive behaviors such as speeding and tailgating. That's because women are more protective. Many women become upset when someone pulls an act while their children are in the vehicle, he said. "I've heard moms say that they drive safer because their children are in the car. Men, in contrast, complain of those who drive while distracted and talk on cell phones, according to the poll. Typically, because men visually see the cell phone in use, they automatically make the assumption that it is interfering with the other driver's ability to operate the vehicle correctly. The male driver is usually more aggressive, when you ask them if they are good drivers, 90 percent of them say they are. Therefore, when they see a source, they see a problem. Distracted drivers pose a major threat on the road, according to 23 percent of those polled. But many adults polled admitted to being distracted themselves, with 54 percent talking on a cell phone, 48 percent changing CDs or DVDs, and 51 percent taking their eyes off the road to deal with children. Distractions aren't the only problem, though. Eighteen percent of Americans polled said aggressive drivers pose the biggest threat on the road, second to drunken drivers. Studies point out that traffic congestions contribute to the behavior, but so do longer commutes and an overall increase in daily stress. People who easily succumb to the stress and pressure of everyday life are taking out their aggressions on the road. They honk their horns, use vulgar language and obscene gestures. There is a certain sense of power and an enormous sense of personal space and safety motorists obtain from driving an automobile. Every day there are cases of irritated drivers, and nearly all drivers have been involved. The irritated actions of drivers jeopardize the safety of all of us.

Afterword

ALTHOUGH MANY TIMES unwanted, irritation is a necessary fact of life. Without irritation, change for the better would never occur. Irritation means that we as humans are paying attention to the stimuli around us. This is important. Survival requires us to be aware of things in our environment. Survival requires cognition. To interact with the world cognitively means to engage our mind. Interacting with our environment allows us the opportunity to create the attitudes, perceptions, and explanations of those things that are around us. The human capacity to understand how our minds work is called *Theory of Mind*. As explained by Rathus (2011) theory of mind refers to the concept that individuals have an experienced-based model of how their minds work. Because many people are put in similar situations, we possess ideas about how we think other people's minds work. This is the reason we become irritated. Our opinions about how other people's minds work causes us to form assumptions about what people will do or how they should behave. When we question why individuals do not behave the way we expect them to, we become irritated. We pre-judge the actions of others based on negative assumptions and when the negative assumptions we make about others are manifested by the actions of the very people we formed the prior opinion about, we become irritated. When others behave in a manner that is not consistent with our expectations we get irritated. The point that is being made here is that expectations and ideas about how other individual's minds work cause us to form opinions based on our perceptions and whether they are justified or refuted will cause us to become irritated. It just depends on how we are feeling that day. Theory of mind also states that adults can learn things in many ways, from observing, performing, hearing, or maybe reading. Theory of mind states that individuals know the difference between subjective perceptions and external objective events, they recognize that appearances may be deceiving. Theory of mind should facilitate a reprieve from the mass irritation prevalent in the human species.

In the final analysis, it can be said that if you read this book and you have agreed with some of the ideas presented, you have been a participant in the act of limbic resonance. As was discussed in the book, limbic resonance occurs when individuals find emotional congruence with others. It is assumed by the author that many of you who read the book and were able to identify with some of the various irritations presented, had similar emotional responses to that of the author and other readers. It is assumed that you have received some form or gratification just knowing that others feel the way you do about certain things.

The inner strain for consistency in the mind of the individual has a significant influence on the potential changes in our attitudes. The inner strain many of us have is influenced by our perceptions. It is useful to know the reasons why we perceive certain situations the way we do, and it is more important that we understand that our perceptions are just that: our *subjective opinion* of an external event or situation. It is important that whatever mental picture we develop based on our perception, we believe it fully. For when we detect inconsistency among our beliefs or attitudes, we experience cognitive dissonance. Cognitive dissonance will cause us to behave in ways that are contrary to our true beliefs. This is dangerous because many of us will irritate others as we perform behaviors that are not reflective of our true selves. You are the existentialist.

Terms Defined

polemic—a piece of writing or a speech in which a person strongly attacks or defends a particular opinion, person, idea or set of beliefs.

luddite—A person opposed to increased industrialization or new technology

existentialism—a 20th century philosophy concerned with human existence, finding self, and the meaning of life through free will, choice, and personal responsibility. Existence precedes essence. The individual is thrown into the world without any previous design of what he or she will become, it is the individual's responsibility to create him or herself and to make him or herself what he or she wants to be.

References

Baines, J. (1995). *Hypsoconsciousness: Teaching For Achieving Personal Success*. New York: John Baines Institute, Inc.

Day, N. (1996). *Sensational TV: Trash or Journalism? (Issues In Focus)*. New Jersey: Enslow Publishing Inc.

Elder, L. & Paul, R. (2003). *How to Detect Media Bias & Propaganda in National and World News*. Dillon Beach, CA: Foundation for Critical Thinking.

Gatto, J. T. (2005). *Dumbing UsDown: The Hidden Curriculum of Compulsory Schooling*. Canada: New Society Publishers.

Hall, J. (2005). *Practically Profound: Putting Philosophy to Work in Everyday Life*. Lanham:Rowman & Littlefield Publishers, Inc.

Hoffer, E. (1951). *The True Believer: Thoughts on the Nature of Mass Movements*. New York: Harper & Row.

Feldman, R. S. (2010). *Psychology and Your Life*. McGraw Hill Learning Solutions.

Green, J. (2007). *Philosophy on the Go*. New York: Fall River Press.

Jones, E. (2008). *My Soul Experience: Moods and Moments*. Authorhouse.

Katz, J. (1999). *How Emotions Work*. Chicago: The University of Chicago Press.

Lakoff, G. (2004). *Don't Think of an Elephant! Know Your Values and Frame the Debate*. Vermont: Chelsea Green.

Lakoff, G. (2008). *The Political Mind: A Cognitive Scientist's Guide to Your Brain and its Politics*. New York: Penguin.

Larson, J. A. (1996). *Steering Clear of Highway Madness: A Driver's Guide to*
Curbing Stress & Strain. Wilsonville: Book Partners.

Law, D.R. (2007). *Briefly: Sartre's Existentialism and Humanism*. London: SCM Press.

Mencken, H. L. (1926). *Notes on Democracy*: A New Edition. New York: Dissident Books.

Newman, J. (2010). Inside the Teenage Brain. Retrieved November 11, 2011, from http://www.parade.com/news/2010/11/28-inside-the-teenage-brain.html.

Ormrod, J. & Rice, F.P. (2002). *Lifespan Development and Learning.* New Jersey: Pearson Custom Publishing.

Postman, N. (2005). *Amusing Ourselves To Death.* New York: Penguin.

Rathus, S. A. (2011). *Childhood and Adolescence:Voyages in Development, Fourth Edition.* Wadsworth Cenage Learning.

Santrock, J.W. (2010), *A topical approach to life span development,* (5th Ed.) New York, NY: McGraw Hill

Vanderbilt, T. (2008). *Traffic: Why We Drive the Way We Do (And What it Says About Us).* Canada: Alfred A. Knopf.

Weiten, W. (1986). *Psychology Applied to Modern Life: Adjustment in the 80s.* California: Brooks/Cole publishing Company.

Warren, E.L. (2012, September/October).Calling a Truce in the Political Wars. *Scientific American Mind.* 23(4), 22-23.

The Accurate & Reliable Dictionary. (2010). Retrieved June. 21,2011, from **http://ardictionary.com/Irritation/7321**

Activist(2009).Howtechnologymakesworkmoreannoying.Retrieved July 25, 2011, from http://hotjobs.yahoo.com/career-articles how_technology_makes_work_more_annoying-1394

All about Philospophy. (2011). Retrieved August 10, 2011, from http://www.allaboutphilosophy.org/existentialism-definition-faq.htm

"Philosophical thinking creates new realities"
—Leonard L. Clark III

www.ingramcontent.com/pod-product-compliance
Lightning Source LLC
Chambersburg PA
CBHW051439280526
45785CB00003B/1358